D0742344

More Scottish than British

The Comparative Territorial Politics Series

Series editors: **Charlie Jeffery**, Professor of Politics, School of Social and Political Science, University of Edinburgh, UK, and **Michael Keating**, Professor of Politics, University of Aberdeen, UK.

Territorial politics is one of the most dynamic areas in contemporary political science. Devolution, regional government and federal reform have reshaped the architecture of government at sub-state and transnational levels, with profound implications for public policy, political competition, democracy and the nature of political community. Important policy fields such as health, education, agriculture, environment and economic development are managed at new spatial levels. Regions, stateless nations and metropolitan areas have become political arenas, contested by old and new political parties and interest groups. All of this is shaped by transnational integration and the rise of supranational and international bodies like the European Union, the North American Free Trade Area and the World Trade Organization.

The *Comparative Territorial Politics* series brings together monographs, edited collections and area studies that further scholarship in the field of territorial politics and policy, decentralization, federalism and regionalism. The series aims to be an outlet for innovative research in this area, grounded in political science, political geography, law, international relations and sociology.

Titles include:

Christopher Carman, Robert Johns and James Mitchell
MORE SCOTTISH THAN BRITISH
The 2011 Scottish Parliament Election

Alain-G Gagnon and Michael Keating (*editors*)
POLITICAL AUTONOMY AND DIVIDED SOCIETIES
Imagining Democratic Alternatives in Complex Settings

Michel Seymour and Alain-G Gagnon (*editors*)
MULTINATIONAL FEDERALISM
Problems and Prospects

Irina Stefuriuc
GOVERNMENT FORMATION IN MULTI-LEVEL SETTINGS
Party Strategy and Institutional Constraints

The Comparative Territorial Politics series
Series Standing Order ISBN 978–0230–29293–2
(*outside North America only*)

You can receive future titles in this series as they are published by placing a standing order. Please contact your bookseller or, in case of difficulty, write to us at the address below with your name and address, the title of the series and the ISBN quoted above.

Customer Services Department, Macmillan Distribution Ltd, Houndmills, Basingstoke, Hampshire RG21 6XS, England

More Scottish than British
The 2011 Scottish Parliament Election

Christopher Carman
Professor of Politics, University of Glasgow, UK

Robert Johns
Senior Lecturer in Politics, University of Essex, UK

James Mitchell
Professor of Public Policy, University of Edinburgh, UK

First published 2014 by
PALGRAVE MACMILLAN

Palgrave Macmillan in the UK is an imprint of Macmillan Publishers Limited, registered in England, company number 785998, of Houndmills, Basingstoke, Hampshire RG21 6XS.

Palgrave Macmillan in the US is a division of St Martin's Press LLC, 175 Fifth Avenue, New York, NY 10010.

Palgrave Macmillan is the global academic imprint of the above companies and has companies and representatives throughout the world.

Palgrave® and Macmillan® are registered trademarks in the United States, the United Kingdom, Europe and other countries.

ISBN 978–1–137–02369–8

This book is printed on paper suitable for recycling and made from fully managed and sustained forest sources. Logging, pulping and manufacturing processes are expected to conform to the environmental regulations of the country of origin.

A catalogue record for this book is available from the British Library.

Library of Congress Cataloging-in-Publication Data
Carman, Christopher J.
    More Scottish than British : the 2011 Scottish Parliament election /
Christopher Carman, Robert Johns, James Mitchell.
        pages cm
    Summary: "With the aid of the most extensive and comprehensive survey data extracted from voters during the 2011 Scottish General, this book analyses the reasons behind why the SNP not only retained their mandate from the people to govern Scotland but further succeeded in winning a resounding majority in the Scottish Parliament. In tackling this overarching question other complex issues are also explored such as whether a pre-occupation with events at Westminster confined the Scottish Elections to the realm of 'second-order' elections? What impact the financial crisis had on elected a parliament that in reality has little economic power? The volume also has a broader appeal to devolved parliamentary elections more broadly by exploring what matters to voters when they cast their ballots for their national parliament in a complex, multi-level Political system. Examining performance evaluations, party loyalties and constitutional preferences, the authors show that Scottish elections are increasingly Scottish affairs, where voters are concerned with government competence – in domestic matters and in managing relations with Westminster." — Provided by publisher.
    ISBN 978–1–137–02369–8 (hardback)
    1. Scotland. Parliament—Elections, 2011.   2. Elections—Scotland.   3. Political parties—Scotland.   4. Scotland—Politics and government—21st century.
    I. Title.
JN1341.C37 2013
324.9411′08612—dc23   2013021790

Contents

Tables and Figures

Tables

Figures

1
The 2011 Scottish Election in Context

The elections to the Scottish Parliament in 2011 were unusual in a number of respects. The Scottish National Party (SNP) was defending a record in government for the first time in its history. It had governed Scotland since 2007 without an overall majority when it won 47 of Holyrood's 129 seats, only winning one more seat than the Labour Party, which until then had governed Scotland in coalition with the Liberal Democrats since the establishment of the Scottish Parliament in 1999. The elections would be a test of both the SNP and minority government. The 2011 elections to Holyrood came a year after elections to the House of Commons, when Labour had been defeated after being in power since 1997. In the three previous Holyrood elections, there had been two years between Westminster and Holyrood elections taking place, which increased the prospect of a spill-over effect from the Westminster elections this time. The formation of a Conservative–Liberal Democrat coalition in London altered the political landscape. Devolution came into being largely in response to the lack of support in Scotland for Conservative governments in the 1980s and 1990s (Denver et al. 2000). The 2011 elections were also the first devolved elections fought against the backdrop of serious economic and fiscal problems. Public expenditure had grown year on year under devolution, in common with spending across the UK, but this had now ended.

These novel aspects of the 2011 Scottish elections created a fascinating context in which to explore political behaviour but also challenges, not least given the need to disentangle the impact of different factors that might each have affected the outcome of the election. Disentangling the variables needs to be combined with understanding the impact each had on other factors. To what extent were expectations of what the Scottish government could deliver altered as a result of the economic crisis? To what extent did the election of a Conservative-led coalition increase the likelihood that the Scottish public would hold the UK government responsible for (prospective) public spending cuts? To what extent did the public take account of the absence of an overall majority in accrediting either blame or credit to the devolved government? This also raises the importance of the previous Scottish elections in 2007 when the SNP emerged with its slight lead over Labour. What expectations did voters have of an SNP government then as compared with 2011? And, of course, the SNP is committed to independence. To what extent and in what ways did the SNP's constitutional position influence voters' behaviour?

These questions were all-important in the Scottish elections but have resonance with questions asked in other liberal democracies, especially with tiered levels of elected government undergoing significant economic and fiscal dislocation. Governments across the world have been adversely affected by economic forces beyond their control but are nonetheless accountable to their electorates. Additionally, a growing literature addresses the impact on political behaviour of multi-tiered systems of representation. Understanding the 2011 Scottish election helps us understand political behaviour beyond Scotland. Equally, this study contributes to the literature on political behaviour in multi-tiered polities especially in the context of fiscal and economic crises.

From coalition to minority government

Vowles has identified two key theories in discussing public perceptions of coalitions, single-party and minority governments: clarity of responsibility and the role of 'veto players' (Vowles 2010: 372). Clarity of responsibility concerns which party or parties are accountable for policy decisions and thereby accountable to the electorate. It is generally assumed that coalition and minority government blur accountability as no single party can be held fully accountable for public policy. Minority government has been described as the least accountable form of government (Powell 2000). Such governments can blame opposition parties for failing to cooperate in pursuit of policy goals. The second theory considers accountability differently. The expectation of 'minimum winning coalitions' (Downs 1962: 47) suggests that coalitions do not require any more parties than would provide the government with a majority. The underlying assumption about minority government is that such governments confront a single majority veto player in opposition. In practice, minority governments may confront a divided opposition. The stability of a minority government will depend on the cohesion of the majority opposition. This is affected by the party system, which is affected in turn by the electoral system.

The Mixed Member Proportional (MMP) electoral system used for Holyrood elections, generally referred to in the UK as the Additional Member System (AMS), has its origins in debates within the Constitutional Convention, a cross/non-party body that formulated the outlines of a scheme of devolution between 1989 and 1992. The system involves voters electing a single district Member of the Scottish Parliament (MSP) in 73 constituencies plus an additional 56 members, seven from each of eight regions. Constituency MSPs are elected using single member districts with a simple plurality, first past the post system. The regional members are elected using closed party lists where members are selected using a system (modified D'Hondt) that takes account of the number of constituency MSPs elected within each region and each party's share of the regional vote, thus providing the Parliament with a degree of proportionality.

The widely held assumption was that AMS would prevent any party having an overall majority. This assumption was based on past performance of the parties, or more specifically the Labour Party, under the simple plurality system in election to the House of Commons. In the first elections to the Scottish Parliament in 1999, Labour achieved an overall majority of constituency MSPs with 53 seats but only 3 list seats, falling 9 seats short of an overall majority. Labour formed a coalition with the Liberal Democrats, providing an overall majority of 8 with 73 seats. The same coalition was formed following the 2003 elections after Labour lost 6 seats, but remained the largest party, and the Liberal Democrats won 17 seats, gaining a constituency seat but consequently losing a list seat. Partnership Agreements between the coalition parties set out the programme for government after 1999 and 2003. But in 2007, when the SNP emerged with its slight lead over Labour, and well short of an overall majority, the Liberal Democrats chose to move out of government. Alex Salmond, as leader of the SNP in Holyrood, defeated Jack McConnell, Labour's leader in the election of Scotland's First Minister by 49 votes to 46 with 33 abstentions. The two Green MSPs voted for Salmond along with the contingent of SNP MSPs. An agreement, short of a coalition, had been reached with the Greens, on three 'core issues': opposition to building new nuclear power stations; agreement to early legislation to reduce climate change pollution annually; and agreement that independence would make Scotland more successful and that the parties would work to 'extend the powers of the Scottish Parliament' (SNP and Greens 2007). These were matters on which the two parties agreed and required no compromises. The Greens agreed to support the minority government 'in votes for First Minister and Ministerial appointments' and the SNP agreed to consult the Green MSPs in advance of each year's legislative and policy programme as well as key measures announced in-year, the substance of the budget and to nominate a Green MSP as convener of a subject committee in the Parliament (SNP and Greens 2007).

In his speech prior to the vote, Alex Salmond had said,

> This Parliament is a proportional Parliament. It is a Parliament of minorities where no one party rules without compromise or concession. The SNP believes that we have the moral authority to govern, but we have no arbitrary authority over this Parliament. The Parliament will be one in which the Scottish Government relies on the merits of its legislation, not the might of a parliamentary majority. The Parliament will be about compromise and concession, intelligent debate and mature discussion. That is no accident. If we look back, we see that it is precisely the Parliament that the consultative steering group – the founding fathers of this place – envisaged.
>
> Official Report Scottish Parliament
> (16 May 2007, col. 24)

The new First Minister discovered the virtues of a proportional Parliament. The much-trumpeted 'new politics', implying a more consensual approach, which some advocates of devolution had hoped would emerge with devolution, was finally becoming a reality. New politics operated alongside typically British adversarial politics within the Holyrood chamber due to the necessity of parliamentary arithmetic rather than a revolution in political attitudes. Westminster-style adversarial politics lived on alongside the need continuously to construct coalitions over the next four years in Holyrood. During election campaigns, parties do not tend to indicate with whom they will coalesce in the event that no party has a majority (Katz 1997: 165–167). Parties in a coalition will each claim primary credit for a popular policy or try to evade responsibility for less popular policies (Gallagher, Laver and Mair 2005), as both Scottish coalition parties did in 2003 on policies such as opposing tuition fees for university students and offering generous 'care for the elderly' policies. It is difficult for a minority government to keep its promises and easier to evade responsibility as it does not have a majority. This might allow it to ditch promises that might have made sense for electoral purposes but proved costly in implementation. Popular SNP manifesto commitments in 2007 included abolishing the council tax and replacing it with a local income tax. Absence of a parliamentary majority prevented this policy chance but, argued the SNP's critics, also meant that the SNP could avoid the troublesome business of introducing a new form of local taxation (Table 1.1).

It has been suggested by a leading scholar of minority government that conventional wisdom associating minority cabinets with 'instability, fractionalization, polarization, and long and difficult formation processes' is a 'historically bounded proposition' (Strøm 1990: 89–90). The UK has experienced minority government at various intervals during the twentieth century: 1910–1915; 1924; 1929–1931; 1974; 1976–1979; 1997. These have usually coincided with periods of economic instability though this coincidence had little to do, at least directly, with minority government. However, this 'historically bounded' association may have coloured expectations of minority government. Strøm's exhaustive analysis of minority government (Strøm 1990) challenges these negative associations, and reminds us of how common minority government is in some parliamentary democracies and that minority can be a rational response by party leaders. David Butler, too, has noted that minority governments outside the UK have proved 'quite stable with few of the dire consequences usually suggested' (Butler 2008: 11). As Strøm notes, minority status allows a government maximum flexibility

Table 1.1 Results of Scottish Parliament elections, 1999, 2003, 2007 and 2011

	Constituencies		Regional lists		Total	
	Votes %	Seats	Votes %	Seats	Seats	Seats %
1999						
Conservative	15.6	0	15.4	18	18	13.9
Labour	38.8	53	33.8	3	56	43.4
Lib Dem	14.2	12	12.5	5	17	13.2
SNP	28.7	7	27.5	28	35	27.1
Green	3.6	11	0.8			
Others	2.7	1	7.2	1	2	1.6
2003						
Conservative	16.6	3	15.5	15	18 (−)	13.9
Labour	34.6	46	29.3	4	50 (−6)	38.8
Lib Dem	15.3	13	11.8	4	17 (−)	13.2
SNP	23.8	9	20.9	18	27 (−8)	20.9
Green	6.9	7	7 (+6)	5.4		
Others	9.7	2	15.8	8	8 (+6)	6.2
2007						
Conservative	16.6	4	13.9	13	17 (−1)	13.2
Labour	32.2	37	29.2	9	46 (−4)	35.7
Lib Dem	16.2	11	11.3	5	16 (−1)	12.4
SNP	32.9	21	31.0	26	47 (+20)	36.4
Green	0.2	0	4.0	2	2 (−5)	1.6
Others	1.9	0	10.6	1	1 (−7)	0.8
2011						
Conservative	13.9	3	12.4	12	15 (+23)	11.6
Labour	31.7	15	26.3	22	37 (−7)	28.7
Lib Dem	7.9	2	5.2	3	5 (−12)	4.8
SNP	45.4	53	44.0	16	69 (+23)	53.5
Green	-	-	4.4	2	2 (n.c.)	1.6
Others	1.1	0	7.7	1	1 (n.c.)	.8

Note: Rounding may result in columns adding to more than 100 per cent.

in seeking support for its policies with shifting coalition strategies, though it also makes them vulnerable to defeat (Strøm 1990: 97). Green-Pedersen also noted, 'shifting coalition strategies offer minority governments optimal conditions for having their policies passed, but it also renders them vulnerable to defeat' (Green-Pederson 2001: 56). Research on how successive Danish minority governments have operated is particularly relevant. Scottish government officials prepared for the possibility of minority government before 2007 by enquiring into the Danish experience.

When a minority government has only one way of building a majority, this gives the supporting opposition party veto powers over individual policies as well as over maintaining the governing party in office. The SNP found itself with limited options in building majorities (see Table 1.2). Minority governments require more than one way of building a majority to maximize its prospects of ensuring its policies pass through parliament. The SNP's advance in 2007 occurred partly due to the decline of the 'Others' but meant that there were fewer means of combining to create a majority in Holyrood. Nonetheless, assuming coherence of party groups in Holyrood, the SNP had five ways of constructing a parliamentary majority after 2007 prior to the appointment of a Conservative MSP as Presiding Officer. Margo MacDonald, the former SNP MSP, sitting as the only Independent since 2003, might prove important in Holyrood votes. The period 2007–2011 would test an inexperienced party governing without a majority. The keys to success for minority governments lie in winning important votes, especially on budgets, but also in an ability to devise policies for which it can claim credit without a parliamentary majority and use existing powers to pursue its policy programme.

Three important caveats have to be noted with respect to majority building. First, much policy-making occurs within the framework of existing legislation and the powers granted to ministers do not require a parliamentary majority. Alex Salmond was keen to quote Donald Dewar, his Labour predecessor as First Minister, who had said: 'As part of the perfectly normal constitutional arrangement, except in certain circumstances, the Scottish Executive is not necessarily bound by resolutions or motions passed by the Scottish Parliament' (Scottish Parliament 31 May 2007). Secondly, theatrical, adversarial politics often hides a willingness to cooperate. This became apparent in annual budget debates during which the minority SNP government had sought to build a parliamentary majority voting in favour of each budget. Labour, the main opposition party, calculated how to oppose each SNP budget formally while, at the same time, ensuring that the SNP government was not brought down by the defeat of the budget. This was highlighted in 2009. Against

Table 1.2 Majority building 1999–2003; 2003–2007; 2007–2011

Majority combinations 1999–2003 Parliament
Labour 56 MSPs requires 9 other for minimum winning coalition

 i. With SNP = 56 + 35
 ii. With LibDems = 56 + 17
 iii. With Conservatives = 56 + 18

SNP 35 MSPs requires 30 others for minimum winning coalition

 i. With Conservative and Liberal Democrats = 35 + 18 + 17

Majority combinations 2003–2007 Parliament
Labour 50 MSPs requires 15 for minimum winning coalition

 i. With SNP = 50 + 27
 ii. With LibDems = 50 + 17
 iii. With Conservatives = 50 + 18
 iv. With Greens, SSP, and three 'Others'* = 50 + 7 + 6 + 3

*This grouping consisted of 4 'Others' in total.
SNP 27 MSPs requires 38 others for minimum winning coalition

 i. With Conservatives+ LibDems+ Greens = 18 + 17 + 7
 ii. With Conservatives+ LibDems+ SSP = 18 + 17 + 6
 iii. With Conservatives+ LibDems + 3 'Others'* = 18 + 17 + 3

*This grouping consisted of 4 'Others' in total.

Majority combinations 2007–2011 Parliament
SNP 47 MSPs requires 18 others for minimum winning coalition.

 i. With Labour 47 + 46
 ii. With Conservatives + Liberal Democrats = 47 + 17 + 16
 iii. With Conservatives + greens = 47 + 17 + 2
 iv. With Conservatives + one other*+ 47 + 17 + 1
 v. With Liberal Democrats + greens = 47 + 16 + 2

Labour 46 MSPs requires 19 others for minimum winning coalition.

 i. With Conservatives + Liberal Democrats = 46 + 17 + 16
 ii. With Conservatives + Greens = 46 + 17 + 2
 iii. With Liberal Democrats + Greens+ Independent = 46 + 16 + 2 + 1

the expectations of all other MSPs, the two Green MSPs decided to join with Labour and Liberal Democrat MSPs to vote against the SNP budget, causing the budget to fall. This would normally precipitate an election but a second budget, almost identical to the first, was proposed, and won the support of Labour and Liberal Democrat MSPs who had opposed the original measure (on the assumption that the Green MSPs would vote for the budget) and thereby allowed the amended budget to pass. Thirdly, and most important in the context of voting behaviour, there is the question of the extent to which the electorate are aware of the existence of, and constraints upon, a minority government. As is well documented in the politics literature, minority governments must build a unique coalition of the willing on each legislative measure put forward. This need to constantly build a voting majority through negotiation and compromise is not something that we would expect the voting public to understand and even consider when evaluating the minority government.

Multi-level elections

The establishment of the Scottish Parliament created a new tier of elected representatives. Public perceptions of the devolved government, especially as it relates to attitudes to the Westminster Parliament and government, can be expected to have influenced political behaviour. A well-established literature on US elections suggests that mid-term elections are quasi-referendums on the federal government and used to punish federal governments (Tufte 1978; Erikson 1988). Much of the work on political behaviour in tiered polities begins with Reif and Schmitt's (1980) work on second-order elections that proposed a series of consequences of elections in which there is 'less at stake':

> Lower levels of participation
> Brighter prospects for small and new political parties
> Higher percentage of invalidated ballots
> and [Central] Government parties lose.

(Reif and Schmitt 1980: 9)

Further work has suggested that subnational elections are not always second order and that there are degrees of 'second-orderness' (Abedi and Siaroff 1999; Hough and Jeffrey 2006; Scully and Elias 2008; McLean et al. 1996; Wyn Jones and Scully 2006). Using Reif and Schmitt's proposed consequences of second order elections, it is less than completely clear how to classify Scottish Parliament elections – while there may be a perception that less is at issue, there is also evidence that Scottish elections are increasingly seen as being consequential, influencing policy in Scotland and the wider UK. While turnout tends to be lower in sub-state elections, this is not always the case. It is not unknown for turnout in some Canadian provinces to be higher than in federal elections including, though not only, Quebec (Studlar 2001). Elections in highly contested polities can produce high levels of turnout, as in Northern Ireland. Henderson and McEwen (2010) found evidence that variations in turnout were affected by two 'region-specific variables': regional attachment and regional autonomy. This argument resembles the view that the 'amount at stake' (Heath et al. 1999) is important. Viewing Scottish Parliament elections in this light (Figure 1.1), the raw turnout numbers would seem to point to Scottish elections being of less than first-order importance. The Scottish public was exuberant in turning out for the first Holyrood elections in 1999, but since then, the percentage of people voting in the Scottish elections has lagged behind those voting in the general election contests.

What is clear is that voters can and do behave differently in statewide and sub-state elections, assuming *ceteris paribus*. However, there are some key differences between how elections are held for Holyrood and Westminster, including the electoral system. The electoral system

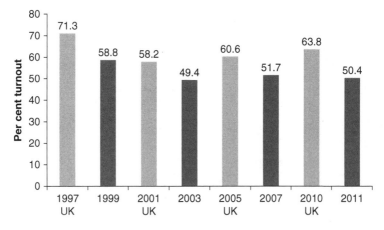

Figure 1.1   Turnout, 1997–2011

has created brighter prospects for small and new political parties and this may be a better explanation than the 'less at stake' explanation. In 2003, the 'Others', that is, parties other than the four main parties with Scottish representation in the House of Commons, performed strongly winning 17 seats (13.2 per cent of the total). However, the small parties owe much to the regional lists – only two 'Others' were elected under the single-member plurality system, and each was an independent rather than a party representative – highlighting the value of the electoral system in ensuring the election of small and new political parties. The Greens now hold a seat in the Commons (for Brighton Pavilion) but their lack of geographically concentrated support in Scotland has led them to contest only the list seats for Holyrood, which they did with much less success in 2007, winning just two seats.

The third criterion, mentioned above, that we might use to consider the 'orderedness' of an election is the relative number of invalidated ballots in the electoral contest. The obvious assumption is that voters who take an election more seriously will attempt to ensure that their ballot is completely and correctly filled in. This, however, could be a crude and error-prone measure of voter interest in an election. For instance, the number of invalidated ballots at Scottish elections rose to unprecedented levels in 2007 but this was not because of voter disinterest, signalling it was a second-order election, but because of ballot paper design (Carman et al. 2008). The structure of the ballot meant that in order to accommodate the excessively long list of parties contesting the regional list, two regions dramatically truncated the instructions on the ballot paper, leading to a much higher percentage of spoiled ballots in those regions (Carman et al. 2008) The number of spoiled ballots in 2011 fell ten fold compared with 2007 (0.42 per cent and 0.34 per cent of constituency and regional list ballots in 2011 compared with 4.08 per cent and 2.88 per cent in 2007) but remained still higher than in Westminster elections. That said, the average number of spoiled ballots per constituency in elections to the House of Commons was generally lower in Scotland than other parts of the UK over elections since 1945. The average number of spoiled papers in Scottish constituency contests in 2005 and 2010 UK elections was 79 and 92 respectively, whereas the average number of spoiled ballots in constituencies for the Holyrood elections in 2011 was 115 but, again, it is unclear whether this was a second-order or electoral system effect or something tied to the different electoral system and ballot structure.

There is a body of work at the other end of the spectrum from the second-order election theory which suggests that elections at sub-state level operate almost in isolation from state-wide politics with minimal central government effects. The notion that 'two political worlds' operate in British Columbia with a 'small world' of provincial politics not affecting and unaffected by the 'larger world' of Canadian politics is used to explain partisan 'inconsistency' (Blake 1982; Blake et al. 1985). This is the behavioural equivalent of the dual, as distinct from interdependent, models of federalism. The dual model 'holds that each level of government, nation and state, is supreme within its area of responsibility. According to this model, neither level is dominant in any general sense, and neither level should interfere in the affairs of the other' (Nice and Fredericksen 1996: 6) while '[...] interdependent models are based on a sharing of power and responsibility, with the various participants often working toward shared goals' (Ibid.: 7–15). Scottish devolution conforms with the latter notion especially regarding fiscal and economic competences though it was conceived in dualist terms (Mitchell 2010a). This interdependence of levels of government may create problems for voters in assigning responsibility across the levels of government. Voters in federal systems do not always attribute responsibility for public policy decisions and their outcomes corresponding well with the formal allocation of competences, suggesting that federal systems create challenges for voters seeking to reward or punish governments for policy outcomes (Cutler 2008). León (2010, 2011) argues that clarity of responsibility requires a vertical distribution of government competences that corresponds with a dual model of tiered government, warning that interdependent models hamper clarity of responsibility. The relationship between decentralization and clarity of responsibilities, according to León, is 'contingent upon the balance of expenditure and fiscal powers across levels of government' resulting in a 'u-shaped' relationship in which citizens are 'better able to ascribe responsibilities in contexts where the level of decentralization is either very low or very high – that is, where there is a level of government that concentrates powers and clearly predominates over the other' (León 2011: 83).

Donald Dewar, who became First Minister at the establishment of devolution, maintained that the Scottish Parliament would allow for 'Scottish solutions to Scottish problems' (Scottish Parliament, 15 June 1999; Dewar 1999). The implication of the rhetoric at the Parliament's inception was that devolved government involved a discrete level of decision-making, free from London interference. The reality in practice has been different largely, not exclusively, due to the financing of devolution that ties the amount of money available to the Scottish Parliament to spending decisions in the rest of the UK. But equally, evidence from the 1997 referendum that approved devolution showed that opposition to London control of Scottish affairs lay behind support for the establishment of a Scottish Parliament (Denver et al. 2000). The evidence from the 2007 Scottish elections suggested that voters were less inclined to vote against the UK central government, though this was a factor, and more willing to consider which party was most likely to be competent in government in Edinburgh (Johns et al. 2010).

It has long been noted in the Canadian and US literature that voters not only vote differently in elections to different levels of government but assume different party identification depending on which level of government is being elected. Party identification was viewed as a long-term psychological attachment in the classic work on party identification (Campbell et al. 1960). This social psychological theory emphasized social structures and socialization in explaining party identification and consequent stability over time. Fiorina (1981) offered an alternative perspective, viewing party identification as rationally constructed and utility-maximizing. Voters are more likely to alter their identification as perceptions of parties retrospectively. Jennings and Niemi (1966) noted that the standard Michigan study question on party identification is 'not directed to any specific level of governmental system' (Jennings and Niemi 1966: 86) but the socialization processes envisaged in the Michigan model would lead us to expect that there should be no differences in party identification in different elections. The federal system and fragmented, decentralized political parties were 'conducive to such splitting of loyalties' (Ibid.: 100). A very high proportion of those with 'mixed-identification pairings' involved an Independent identification at one level or other (Ibid.: 88). Having a party/Independent mixed identification might indicate a weakened version of party identification whereas the less prevalent identification involving two different parties may be qualitatively different. Stewart and Clarke (1998) explain this 'inconsistent' partisan identity in terms of the 'evaluative theory of party identification' meaning simply that voters alter their identities according to existing or prospective evaluations. We return to the question of multi-level party identification in Chapter 5.

For now, we want to raise the possibility that the 2011 Scottish parliamentary elections might be expected to have been affected by the UK level more than previous devolved elections for a number of reasons. First, there was only one year between the UK and Scottish elections and the UK elections resulted in the first change of government at Westminster since devolution, bringing back to power – though as the main party in a coalition rather than with an overall majority – the party that Scots reacted against in their support for devolution more than a decade before. Following the 2010 general election, as Figure 1.2 indicates, the Holyrood voting intention polls saw a decided shift toward Labour – the main opposition party to the Conservative-Liberal Democrat coalition in Westminster.

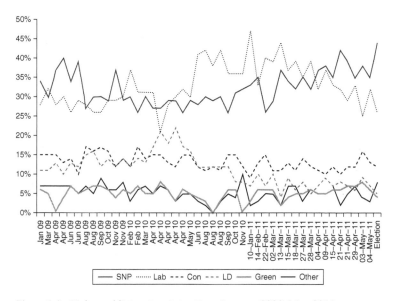

Figure 1.2   Holyrood list voting intention, January 2009–May 2011

One reading of these post-2010 election polls suggests that the UK dimension became uppermost in the Scottish electorate's mind as attention was focused on political events in London. That is, the UK dimension seemed to spill over into Holyrood voting intentions for a period. It was not until the 2011 Holyrood campaign was in full swing, about a month before the May 2011 election, that the aggregate voting intentions began to reflect what we would think of as the 'Scottish dimension' (with the SNP assuming the lead over Labour). We return to the relative importance of the 'Scottish dimension' throughout this book, but pay it special attention in Chapter 4.

Economic and fiscal crisis

In the previous section we discussed the blurring of responsibility that occurs with minority government. A further blurring of responsibility occurs when responsibility for economic and political outcomes is unclear to voters. A growing literature attempts to assess the importance of globalization on the vote. Hellwig argues that voters will evaluate political parties differently when parties are perceived to be constrained by exogenous economic factors. Voters compensate for this lack of responsibility by adjusting the criteria on which they evaluate political actors and increase the salience of non-economic factors (Hellwig 2008). Extending this argument to sub-state governments, it is similarly likely that voters might adjust evaluation criteria by prioritizing non-economic factors to account for the limitations imposed by globalization and central governments.

Scholars have highlighted implications of the overall context of globalization and public perceptions of governmental responsibility for economic management. Hyper-globalists suggest the end of the state (Ohmae 1990; Horsman and Marshall 1994) while more 'moderate' globalists view state autonomy as diminished, constraining the state's policy-making capacity (Friedman 1999; Scholte 2000). National governments, it is maintained, are no longer the 'locus of effective political power' (Held and McGrew 1998: 242). An alternative view challenges the powerlessness of states (Weiss 1998; also Weiss 2003 for debate). What concerns us is how the electorate perceives the impact of globalization on responsibility. At best, it has been argued, the evidence is ambivalent on whether citizens perceive constraints that are claimed to exist to limit political leaders' abilities to 'make a difference' (Vowles 2008). Voters would not rationally blame governing parties for economic conditions that were not caused by governing parties (Duch and Stevenson 2008).

The Scottish block grant providing finance for the Scottish Parliament increased by 60 per cent in real terms between 1999 and 2010, amounting to annual average increases of 5 per cent. This context of ever-increasing growth in spending was abruptly halted following the economic and fiscal crises that occurred over the months following the 2007 election. Difficulties in managing Scottish finances had been anticipated even before the crisis. A report produced in July 2006, but only published after the 2007 election, reviewed Scottish Executive budgets and concluded that the Partnership Agreement between Labour and the Liberal Democrats setting out priorities had been agreed in a 'relatively benign economic climate where there was little evidence of pressure on public sector spending. The next PA is unlikely to be set in such a benign economic climate' (Howat 2006: 4.2.3). There would be no Partnership Agreement in 2007 as the SNP governed as a minority but the benign climate had gone. The economic and fiscal crises significantly exacerbated these problems. In 2010, the Auditor General for Scotland, charged with auditing Scottish public bodies, referred to a 'long hard financial winter' (Black 2010). An Independent Budget Review (IBR) panel established by the Scottish government, at the insistence of the Conservative opposition in Holyrood, produced a sobering report in July 2010 (Beveridge 2010). The IBR set out public spending and public policy options in the context of the tightened fiscal environment. It noted that it was reporting less than a year before the Holyrood elections,

> The pre-election period, though a natural opportunity to debate matters of public policy, inevitably heightens the risk that short-term political imperatives polarize national discourse and exaggerate differences of approach. Given the seriousness of the current fiscal situation, and the high degree of consensus evident in representations to the Review, the Panel would strongly encourage the maximum degree of frankness and cross-party agreement about the scale of the problem, potential solutions and the necessity to act now
>
> (Beveridge 2010: 1.2.7)

The campaign

Labour was ahead in the polls for much of the year prior to May 2011, leading commentators to predict a change of government at Holyrood. The Liberal Democrats were signalling support for a return to coalition with Labour, and the Greens were signalling a willingness to work with Labour. But as the election approached, the polls shifted in favour of the SNP (see Figure 1.2). By 23 March, the last day the Parliament sat before the election, the SNP had pulled ahead and this lead increased over the course of the following weeks leading up to polling day. As has become standard in Holyrood elections, there were a number of leadership debates with the four main party leaders: Alex Salmond of the SNP, Iain Gray of Labour, Annabel Goldie of the Conservatives and Tavish Scott of the Liberal Democrats (see Chapter 3). Manifestos were launched during the campaign with more similarities than differences between the parties on substantive public policies, other than the constitution. The SNP argued for a referendum on independence, which was opposed by all other parties represented in Holyrood after 2007 except the Greens. Some months before the election, Labour abandoned its opposition to a council tax freeze and promised that a Labour Government would freeze council tax for two years. It also mimicked the SNP in supporting free university education. However, the SNP promised to freeze the council tax for the duration of the Parliament, thus outbidding Labour while Labour was unable to criticize the policy in principle. Each party promised to increase police numbers and all but the Liberal Democrats supported the creation of a single police force. Labour promised to reinstate a plan to link Glasgow Central and Glasgow airport by rail, end youth unemployment through an apprenticeship scheme and introduce mandatory six-month prison sentences for people found in possession of knives. Of the four main parties, the Conservatives stepped outside the policy mainstream more than the others, promising to reintroduce prescription charges, which had been abolished by the SNP, give support to building new nuclear power stations, introduce a variable university graduate fee and replace community service with short prison sentences.

In 2007, voters were attracted to the SNP's positive campaigning and put off by a perceived negativity in Labour's campaign (Pattie et al. 2011). Once more, the overall perception was that the SNP fought a positive campaign, even more so than in 2007 while Labour particularly was perceived to have been negative in its campaign tone (see Chapter 3). If we measured how important an election was to a party by the amount spent on its election campaign, then it would appear that this was a first-order election for the SNP. Against the backdrop of having fought a UK general election campaign in 2010 and a difficult economic climate, it was to be expected that the parties would have less available to fight the 2011 campaign. This pattern is revealed in Table 1.3, with only the Greens increasing their campaign spending over the 2007 campaign. As in 2007, the SNP outspent the other parties though less than it had spent four years previously but closer to its previous figure than was achieved by the other parties. This meant that the SNP spent three-quarters of the legal limit permitted, whereas Labour spent just over half the amount it was legally entitled to spend. The SNP had spent only £315,776 in 2010 (Electoral Commission 2011), 28 per cent of the amount it spent in 2011. In 2011, the Conservatives spent a fifth of the amount it had spent at the previous year's UK election. Labour spent less in 2011 than in 2010 though the difference was much smaller than the Conservative or SNP margins and the Liberal Democrats spent under 40 per cent of the amount they had spent in 2010.

Looking at where the campaigns devoted their resources in Tables 1.4 and 1.5, we see further evidence that all of the parties shifted their campaign strategies from 2007. Reflecting the decreasing importance of the parties' political broadcasts, all of the parties, aside from the Greens, decreased the amount they spent on their party broadcasts. On the other hand, most of the parties (aside from the Conservatives) increased the amount devoted to sending mailings through prospective voters' letterboxes, while at the same time decreasing their general advertising budgets. On the surface, this would seem to mirror a general trend in British elections – the increased targeting of specific sets of voters and a decline in broad, generalized campaigning (Denver, Carman and Johns 2012).

Overall, the general campaign was fairly low key with the usual stage-managed events organized by the parties. One of the few moments when a party lost control of such an event occurred early in the campaign. Iain Gray was at Glasgow Central train station to highlight the SNP government's decision to cancel a planned rail link to Glasgow airport when he was 'ambushed' by a group calling itself

Table 1.3 2011 Campaign spending in Scottish elections compared to Westminster (general) elections, in GBP

	Holyrood 2003	Westminster 2005	Holyrood 2007	Westminster 2010	Holyrood 2011	2011–2007 Change in £	2011 Spending as a percent of 2007 (%)
Conservative	323,279	1,317,192	601,982	1,273,110	273,462	-328,520	45
labour	726,702	1,636,450	1,102,866	967,904	816,889	-285,977	74
Lib Dems	130,360	435,406	297,572	470,619	176,300	-121,272	59
Greens	63,864	0	99,132	0	132,464	33,332	134
SNP	473,107	193,987	1,382,730	315,776	1,141,662	-241,068	83
Other parties	354,853	83,135	576,242	63,135	90,469	-485,773	16
Total	2,072,165	3,666,170	4,060,524	3,090,544	2,631,246		

Source: Electoral Commission (2012).

Table 1.4 2011 Party spending by expenditure category

	Conservatives		Labour		Lib Dems		Scottish Greens		SNP	
	2007	2011	2007	2011	2007	2011	2007	2011	2007	2011
Party political broadcasts	29,338	5088	59,685	46,236	15,381	4558	3161	7630	90,726	71,961
Advertising	119,419	664	337,609	115,986	26,166	8441	28,979	10,699	494,642	294,601
Unsolicited material to electors	247,521	200,150	270,020	545,746	98,323	104,274	35,947	73,572	323,580	405,728
Manifesto or referendum material	9134	4062	17,525	9147	6905	1972	7111	2665	56,999	14,067
Marketing research/ canvassing	15,353	1434	107,477	32,623	64,626	20,680	2199	1860	178,705	201,613
Media	17,957	1922	29,710	6153	29,481	73	3855	14,123	45,041	32,269
Transport	2243	10,475	72,366	16,799	29,635	10,530	565	951	52,239	34,957
Rallies and other events	270	1783	89,685	19,693	1710	1936	2036	194	64,652	20,689
Overheads/general administration	160,747	47,884	118,789	24,503	25,345	23,836	15,279	20,771	76,146	65,777

Source: Electoral Commission (2012).

Table 1.5 2011 Party spending by expenditure category as a percentage of 2007 spending

	Conservatives (%)	Labour (%)	Lib Dems (%)	Greens (%)	SNP (%)
Party political broadcasts	17.3	77.5	29.6	241.4	79.3
Advertising	0.6	34.4	32.3	36.9	59.6
Unsolicited material to electors	80.9	202.1	106.1	204.7	125.4
Manifesto or referendum material	44.5	52.2	28.6	37.5	24.7
Marketing research/ canvassing	9.3	30.4	32.0	84.6	112.8
Media	10.7	20.7	0.2	366.4	71.6
Transport	467.0	23.2	35.5	168.3	66.9
Rallies and other events	660.4	22.0	113.2	9.5	32.0
Overheads/general administration	29.8	20.6	94.0	135.9	86.4

Source: Electoral Commission (2012).

'Citizens United Against Cuts to Public Services'. Mr Gray and his team of Labour members sought refuge in a nearby fast-food outlet only to be followed by the protesters and the media, creating scenes that allowed his opponents to characterize Mr Gray as running away from a difficult situation. The Conservatives also suffered an early embarrassment in the campaign when three of the party's candidates withdrew, including one who accused the party of forcing him out to make way for Ruth Davidson, who would become leader shortly after the election.

In 2007, the SNP was endorsed by a number of newspapers but the large circulation papers had continued to back Labour. The front page of the Scottish edition of *The Sun* in 2007 had shown a picture of a noose with the words, 'VOTE SNP TODAY AND YOU PUT SCOTLAND'S HEAD IN THE NOOSE' followed by a series of pages offering, 'Reasons to be fearful'. By 2011, *The Sun* had decided that the SNP was to be trusted and while it made it clear that it opposed independence, its front-page headline on 19 April read, 'PLAY IT AGAIN SALM', followed by six pages of support for the SNP, especially First Minister Alex Salmond, and excoriation of Labour. It printed a picture of its front page from four years before and explained why it had changed its mind. As Scotland's largest selling newspaper, with 330,000 sales, this was a major boost to the SNP.

Conclusion

The Scottish electorate was faced with choices made difficult with the blurring of accountability in a number of ways. Minority government gives the governing party scope to blame its opponents for blocking its policy programme. Devolved government further blurs lines of accountability, especially given the financing of devolution. The global financial crisis has been used by governments of all hues around the world to shift responsibility for poor economic performance away from those heading governments. Voters might have been inclined to judge the governing party at Holyrood or the governing parties at Holyrood or even pass judgement on the previous UK Labour Government. Whoever won the election would face unprecedented difficulties managing economic and fiscal difficulties under devolution, indeed with the prospect of public spending cuts unprecedented in modern UK politics. The constitutional question has long been a feature of Scottish elections but its impact on the election was unclear. The SNP's commitment to independence had been played down in successive Holyrood elections, largely by a commitment to hold a referendum on independence, de-coupling or at least diluting the connection between a vote for the SNP from a vote for independence. After four years of an SNP Government that had been unable to pass legislation to hold a referendum, this de-coupling may have appeared to have succeeded.

In the following chapters, we develop an explanation of how Scotland votes today. More accurately, we develop an explanation of what motivates Scottish voters voting in Scottish elections. We begin this explanation in Chapter 2 with a discussion of the classic sources of variation in Scottish voting behaviour: demographic differences, religious differences and class differences. We find that these variables are proving less useful than they used to be in delineating different voters – Labour and SNP voters, for instance, are very hard to distinguish by class and religious background.

With the traditional dividing lines between voters becoming blurred, in the following chapters we turn to other possible variables we can use to predict how (and why) Scottish voters vote as they do in Holyrood elections. In Chapter 3 we address the pivotal role that parties and leaders play in helping to formulate voters' electoral decisions. In many ways, this chapter deals with the question of why the dominant position that Labour has long enjoyed in Scottish politics did not equate to a Scottish Labour Government being returned following the 2011 election. Turning that question on its head, we also address how the SNP's minority government managed to overcome the 'costs of ruling' and produce such a resounding victory. The unsurprising answer lies in the fact that the SNP had, in Alex Salmond, the most popular and most influential leader, and that the party had cultivated an image of competence, trustworthiness and commitment to stand up for Scotland's interests within the UK.

Chapter 4 delves more deeply into the importance of public perceptions of the parties' capacities to deal with the important issues facing Scotland. Since the main parties did not much distinguish themselves from one another in terms of their stances on the main policy questions of the day, the electorate was left to focus on the issues on which there is agreement about outcomes but not necessarily about who is best placed to achieve that outcome. Here we find that the SNP managed to secure its landslide victory through one of the most prosaic of reasons – it was seen as the party most competent to govern. Yet, and importantly, it is also clear that the SNP's victory was not a ringing endorsement of the one major policy that distinguishes the party from the other 'leading' Holyrood parties. We use our panel data to demonstrate that, while voters' constitutional preferences may have led some to vote for the SNP in 2007, the 2011 vote showed little sign of being swayed by constitutional politics. Indeed, it seems that the 2007–2011 SNP minority government may have eased some voters' fears and concerns about the SNP's independence agenda.

This leads us to address the particular 'Scottish dimension' of the 2011 Scottish elections and brings us back to the question: After three full sessions of the Scottish Parliament, how much do voters feel is at stake in Scottish Parliament elections? We would imagine that, as the Scottish public increasingly comes to grips with devolution and better understands the ebb and flow of Holyrood politics, voters would increasingly develop uniquely Scottish political identities. This is confirmed in Chapter 5. Even the economy, ostensibly a domain in which Westminster rather than Holyrood pulls the levers, became in many respects a 'Scottish' issue in 2011 as the parties fought over who could best insulate Scotland against the chill wind of fiscal austerity blowing from London. We argue that Scottish voters face two political worlds and, because Scottish Parliament elections take place in a now distinct devolved world, they are becoming increasingly 'Scottish'. The notion of parallel political worlds is supported by evidence from a survey experiment embedded within the Scottish Election Study (SES), which shows that the patterns of party identification within the Scottish electorate depend heavily on whether respondents are primed to think about 'UK politics at Westminster' or 'Scottish politics at Holyrood'. These differences go a long way to explaining why the 2010 and 2011 elections, while just one year apart, saw such dramatically different outcomes in Scotland.

In Chapter 6 we pull together the different influences on voter choice in Scottish Parliament elections discussed in the previous chapters into a single statistical model of party choice in the 2011 Scottish parliament elections. Our models largely reinforce the 'performance politics' (or 'valence') model of party choice: voters are largely influenced by their evaluations of relative party (and government) competence. Tied to this, leader evaluations came to play a role in the election, where Alex Salmond's appeal to voters helped the SNP to victory. Perhaps as interesting as the variables that are significant predictors of party choice in the 2011 election are those dogs that barked only quietly, such as constitutional preferences. As we highlight several times throughout this book, in 2011 Scots were, by and large, voting for the SNP as a Scottish government, not as a route to independence.

2
Results and the Sources of Party Support

In this chapter we will use data from the 2011 SES to consider who votes for the various parties, the impact that the electoral system had on the outcome, the relationship between constituency and list voting and how voters' allegiances shifted over time. In essence, the chapter aims to describe the typical voter for each of the main parties. In the past, this was deemed a relatively easy task but this election has shown that it is less easy to distinguish between the main parties in terms of socio-economic backgrounds. The biggest shock of the election was the overall majority won by the SNP, a result that was widely viewed as highly unlikely. The mixed-member proportional electoral system used in Scottish Parliamentary elections had had an immediate impact from the first Holyrood elections in 1999 when Labour, by far the main beneficiary of the simple plurality system, was predictably unable to command an overall majority and formed two consecutive coalition governments with the Liberal Democrats. Leading into the 2011 election, while some commentators may have expected that the SNP might retain or strengthen its positions as Scotland's largest party, few anticipated that it would have an overall majority. We will explore how this was achieved under a system assumed by its designers to be almost impossible. We will also consider how voters shifted allegiances from 2007, when the SNP won its one-seat advantage over Labour, through the 2010 UK general election, which saw Labour not only win a convincing overall majority of Scottish seats but witnessed an increase in its Scottish support while its vote south of the border declined. We are able to follow the views of a panel of the same voters to track these changes in political behaviour.

Scottish Election Study (SES), 2011

The analyses we present in this and the following chapters make extensive use of data collected for the 2011 SES. The Economic and Social Research Council-funded 2011 SES was a large survey designed specifically to assist academics, practitioners and the public to better understand how the Scottish electorate perceives and understands elections to the Scottish Parliament. The specific technical information about the pre- and post-wave surveys – including sampling information, fieldwork dates, survey instrument construction and so on – is provided in Appendix 1. There are, however, several aspects of the 2011 SES that we should elaborate on before we turn to our analyses of the data: namely, the survey mode and the SES's inter- and intra-panel design.

First, as it did in 2007, the SES contracted with YouGov to conduct the election study over the internet. The main reason for conducting the SES online is, of course, cost. It is significantly less expensive to conduct surveys online than it is to conduct face-to-face surveys. As in all things, however, there are trade-offs between the two methods of survey administration. While internet surveys are substantially less expensive to conduct, they do tend to be somewhat less accurate in replicating known turnout parameters. Generally speaking, a well-designed face-to-face survey can do a better job of replicating differences in turnout across groups than can an equally well-designed internet survey. That said, face-to-face surveys, in addition to being extremely expensive to conduct, tend to be a rather lethargic method of gathering public opinion data. As long as there are public opinion scholars – and, more importantly, firms that profit by conducting surveys on behalf of those scholars – there is likely to be an active debate on the 'best' mode for surveying large populations. Indeed there is already an extensive literature on the subject. Looking specifically to compare different survey modes used in Scotland, Johns et al. (2007), compared predictions derived from the 2007 SES and the 2007 Scottish Social Attitudes survey, both conducted following the 2007 Holyrood election. While they find that the internet survey did over-report turnout (though the difference between the surveys was not statistically significant), their analysis shows little difference in the main predictors of party choice. Where they do identify differences in prediction, these seem to be due to the fact that the

SSA's face-to-face interviews were held several weeks after the election. They conclude that, as long as we recognize their weaknesses, there is much to recommend internet surveys as a (relatively) inexpensive method for capturing responses much sooner after an event (such as an election), than face-to-face surveys.

Using the internet as the mode for administering the SES allowed us to include multiple panels in the 2011 study. Following what has become the common practice for election studies, the 2011 SES included a pre- and post-election panel. That is, the same respondents were surveyed the week before the election and then again in the two weeks following the election. The key advantage of this design in 2011 is that it allows us to analyse party choice – that is, the vote – based on information gathered before our respondents went to the polls. This helps us deal with the problem of survey respondents adjusting their responses to survey questions to match their vote choice. For instance, we could imagine that a respondent who decided to cast a vote for, say, the SNP, would adjust their responses to questions asking about issues closely identified with the SNP – for example, constitutional issues – to more closely align with their perceptions of the SNP's positions. By asking about relevant issues and controversies prior to the election, and using those responses to predict vote choice, we are able to deal with the problem of respondents aligning their personal policy preferences with their vote choice after the fact.

Using YouGov's pool of respondents, the SES was able to constitute a 'panel' with responses from the 2007 election study. That is, since YouGov uses a unique identifier for the respondents in their pool, the 2011 study was able to return to respondents from the 2007 study. This creates a somewhat unique Scottish data set – respondents interviewed in two consecutive election studies were asked a wide swathe of questions about party preferences, issue positions and constitutional dispositions as well as the usual battery of election-related questions. Leveraging these data, we are able to compare individual responses to these questions across election cycles, examining the (in)stability of individual issue positions and vote choice over time.

Socio-demography of the Scottish vote

Parties draw support unevenly from the electorate, differing in terms of class, religion, age, gender and geography. Core support provides parties with an important electoral base but parties seeking to maximize electoral support need to build beyond that core. Analysing our data, we are able to paint a picture of the kind of voters most likely to vote for each of the main parties and how this has changed over time. While this tells us who votes for whom, this does not tell us *why* they vote in this way but may provide some clues. An earlier generation of psephologists focused heavily on societal cleavages. In a widely quoted statement, Lazarsfeld, Berelson and Gaudet maintained that, 'a person thinks, politically, as he is, socially. Social characteristics determine political preference' (Lazarsfeld, Berelson and Gaudet 1968: 27). This has often been interpreted as a determinist view of political behaviour but only when read out of context, as Zuckerman pointed out (Zuckerman 2005: 6). Lazarsfeld, Berelson and Gaudet had noted the *tendency* rather than the certainty of social contextual influence and that people 'belong to a variety of groups' and it was unclear 'with *which group*' they are most likely to vote (Lazarsfeld et al. 1968: 170). Whether expressed in determinist terms or only as a tendency, the key point was that social structures had a significant influence on political behaviour.

In their historical work on social cleavages, Lipset and Rokkan argued that two critical junctures in European history had given rise to societal cleavages with path-dependent qualities: the 'national' revolution when states were formed led to a centre-periphery cleavage and a church-state cleavage, as emerging central governments competed for the loyalties and asserted authority over populations across the state; the 'industrial' revolution which gave rise to class and urban-rural cleavages. They maintained that, 'the party systems of the 1960s reflect, with few but significant exceptions, the cleavage structures of the 1920s [...] [T]he party alternatives, and in remarkably many cases, the party organizations, are older than the majorities of the national electorates' (Lipset and Rokkan 1967: 50). Rose and Urwin (1970) provided confirmation of this 'freezing hypotheses' in Western Europe, suggesting that the 'first priority of social scientists is to explain the *absence* of change' (Rose and Urwin 1970: 295).

Much was to change in understandings of political behaviour over the next decade. But the question at this point in time was which cleavage was most important. In an earlier publication, Rose and Urwin argued that religious divisions 'not class, are the main social bases of parties in the Western world today' (Rose and Urwin 1969: 12); across most of Europe, only in the Scandinavian states and Britain was class found to be more useful than religion in predicting left-right party choice (Rose 1974: 16–18). A rather parochial British perspective viewed class as all-important, mixed with a tendency to ignore the territorial dimension of voting behaviour. Class may have been very significant in Scottish electoral politics but to argue that all else was merely embellishment oversimplified the analysis. While social class was the 'strongest influence upon voting choice [...] other influences may not be so totally eclipsed by class in Scotland as the theory of British homogeneity maintains' (Budge and Urwin 1966: 50).

As voting patterns show, even accounting for class, there was a distinct pattern to political behaviour in Scotland compared to other parts of Britain, whether this was a manifestation of the centre-periphery cleavage or a manifestation of other social differences. Religion, for example, has had enduring significance in Scottish political behaviour (Bochel and Denver 1970; Budge and Urwin 1966; Budge et al. 1972). However, the religious dimension to Scottish electoral behaviour did not conform to the classic cleavage model devised by Lipset and Rokkan (Lipset and Rokkan 1967). The cleavage manifested itself less as a clerical vs. anti-clerical divide in voting behaviour, instead manifesting as an inter-denominational (Catholic/Protestant) cleavage. Labour appealed more to Catholics and the Conservatives and Liberals to Protestants, giving them significant core supporters especially when combined with class identity. Moving beyond a basic examination of denominational divides, it is now widely acknowledged in the comparative study of religion and political behaviour that the religious cleavage has two dimensions: the religion or denomination to which voters belong (or whether they have any religious affiliation at all); and the degree of religiosity (Dalton 1996: 177–179). Beyond religion, there was some additional evidence of an urban-rural divide in Scottish voting behaviour though this manifestation of another of the Lipset and Rokkan cleavages may have owed much to class identities. In essence, even at the high point when class dominated understandings of *British* electoral politics there was evidence that much else needed to be taken into account in understanding *Scottish* politics.

In the 2011 election, the old cleavages remained relevant but were much less useful in helping us distinguish between the main parties than they have been in the past. As the SES data reveals, in large measure this was due to increasing similarities (or decreasing differences) in the compositions of SNP and Labour supporters compared to previous electoral cycles. The SNP advanced among all groups but notably so among those social groups from whom it had previously struggled to win support. At first glance, it appeared that the SNP had broken through Labour's classic citadels by winning more support among the subjective working-class Catholics and in urban Scotland. An additional distinguishing characteristic of the SNP vote, and its membership more specifically, as shown in other research (Johns et al. 2011), was gender. Previously, the party's advances, and particularly in 2007, had been associated with its advantage among men. But in 2011, it increased its support among women to a greater extent and largely removed the gender gap that had previously existed. Labour now appears to have a greater gender gap but in the opposite direction.

But there are several important observations that should be emphasized. First, the SNP's support rose among all social groups. Looking at Table 2.1 and more specifically the column denoting the change in SNP support (i.e., its share of the list, or regional, vote) between 2007 and 2011, we see a full slate of positive figures to the SNP's advantage. This is the proverbial rising tide that raises all of the ships. The SNP's appeal may have differed across social groups, suggesting that social structure still matters in some way, but *there were no major groups in which the SNP failed to improve its appeal*. This suggests that social structural explanations are likely to be inadequate in explaining the outcome of the 2011 election. Perhaps more importantly, this also means that it is now more difficult to predict an individual's voting behaviour based on socio-demographic characteristics in Scotland than at any previous time.

Secondly, while the SNP may have become the most popular party among Catholics, for example, we should heed the distinction found in the comparative literature between religious affiliation and religiosity, or the intensity of religious belief and practice in one's life. Table 2.2 presents the list vote by both religious affiliation and religiosity. Here, we classified respondents who say that they attend churches services at least once a fortnight as being 'religious', compared to identifiers who attend services less often.[1] As Table 2.2

Table 2.1 List vote by demographic group, 2011 and change 2007–2011

	2011				Change 2007–2011			
	Cons	Lab	Lib Dem	SNP	Cons	Lab	Lib Dem	SNP
Sex								
Male	12	24	6	46	−2	−5	−4	+11
Female	12	29	4	43	−2	−1	−9	+16
Age								
18–34	7	24	8	43	−6	−9	−3	+17
35–54	10	28	4	47	−	−2	−8	+16
55+	17	26	5	42	−2	−1	−5	+7
Residence								
Urban	11	28	4	43	−1	−6	−7	+15
Rural	14	25	6	45	−5	+6	−7	+8
Social class								
A, B	14	25	5	41	−4	−3	−7	+15
C1	17	25	8	41	+5	−3	−5	+9
C2, D, E	9	28	4	47	−	−6	−3	+9
Religion								
None	9	25	5	47	−4	−2	−8	+15
Church of Scotland	15	26	6	44	−	−2	−4	+9
Catholic	9	36	2	43	−1	−10	−3	+15

Table 2.2 List vote by religion and religiosity

	Secular	Catholic		Church of Scotland		Other Protestant	
		Religious	Cultural	Religious	Cultural	Religious	Cultural
DNV	19	12	19	8	13	6	15
Conservative	7	5	8	19	12	33	21
Labour	18	35	23	14	20	12	21
Lib Dem	4	0	2	6	5	6	6
SNP	36	36	38	42	40	22	28
Other	16	12	9	12	10	22	1
N	989	58	107	61	302	51	102

shows, more religious Catholics were significantly less likely to shift away from Labour than 'cultural Catholics', those who may have been born in the faith but do not practice their faith on a regular basis. This conforms with earlier understandings of voting behaviour discussed above in which it was found that those with a stronger sense of community, or communion, within a social group will be least likely to shift political allegiance. It was among cultural Catholics that the SNP has seen its greatest advances over a long period of time, but most notably in 2011.

Similarly, Labour retains its core support among those with the strongest identification with class. Indeed, one of the clearest aspects to shine through the analysis of social class and the Labour vote is the distinct and clear differences in objective and subjective social class. Here we use the standard NRS (A, B, C1, C2, D and E) 'social grade', or class, scale as the 'objective' indicator (where this scale is based on employment or job function). For the subjective indicator we use the question from the post-election wave that simply and straightforwardly put it to respondents, 'Most people say they belong either to the middle class or the working class. If you *had* to make a choice, which would you say that you belong to?' Respondents were given the options 'Middle class', 'Working class' and 'Can't choose'.

Using these two indicators, Table 2.3 presents the differences in regional vote by where the objective measure places respondents (with C2, D and E being classified as 'working class') and where they place themselves on the subjective measure.

One of the interesting blocks here is the one in which respondents objectively fall into the 'working class' but subjectively identified

Table 2.3 Party vote by objective and subjective social class, column percentages

		Subjective		
		Middle	Working	
Objective	Middle	28	9	Conservative
		19	34	Labour
		10	4	Lib Dem
		43	52	SNP
		277	*271*	*N*
	Working	22	8	Conservative
		19	33	Labour
		9	4	Lib Dem
		50	55	SNP
		126	445	*N*

themselves with the 'middle' class. The only difference between these respondents and those who both objectively and subjectively fell in the middle-class category is a slight shift from Conservative voting toward SNP voting. The same percentage (19 per cent) in the working/middle category said that they voted Labour as in the middle/middle category. The shift in the Labour vote is between the subjective and objective working-class classifications. Those respondents self-identifying as 'working class' showed a much greater inclination to vote Labour than those who said that they are middle class. Reports of the death of social cleavages may be exaggerated (Elff 2007: 289). That said, referring back to Table 2.1, the evidence in Scotland suggests that the core vote has shrunk and that parties must now work much harder to build beyond this core.

From class to national identity

While socio-economic structures gave rise to these changes, they involved a sense of collective identity. Cleavages are important electorally so long as they have distinct social bases, members have a sense of collective identity and party organizations are organized around these cleavages (Gallagher et al. 2006: 268–269). In this sense, class is as much an 'imagined community' as is national identity (Anderson 1991). Changes in electoral behaviour in the 1970s suggested a thawing of the social structural explanations. A new orthodoxy challenged the importance of structural explanations of voting behaviour. The 'decline of class voting in Britain' (Franklin 1985) was thought to lead to unpredictable election outcomes (Crewe 1982). This finding in British electoral politics was evident elsewhere (Franklin et al. 1992; Dalton 2002) though others challenged this new emerging orthodoxy (Bartolini and Mair 1990). This thaw created opportunities for new and smaller parties. Indeed, it was conceivable that the thawing of one form of collective identity created opportunities for alternative identities to arise. This thaw, or de-alignment, focused almost exclusively on class when discussing social structural and electoral behaviour, though also included party de-alignment, but established parties benefited from other alignments too. As we can see, there has been a significant religious de-alignment in Scotland.

There have been attempts to explain the rise of the SNP as the rise in importance of the centre-periphery cleavage. However, the extent of the thaw should not be exaggerated. The emerging SNP struggled to break into these more aligned sections of the community (Miller 1981: 146). In 1979, Labour won 67 per cent of the Scottish Catholic vote (cf 42 per cent of overall vote) while the Conservative support among Protestants was 39 per cent (cf 31 per cent of overall vote) suggesting the persistence of a religious denominational cleavage.

In the 1980s, Labour's support in Scotland held up well compared with its decline south of the border. A higher proportion of Scottish voters recorded both a class and national identity in 1992 than in 1979 (Brand et al. 1993) creating a 'distinctive form of politics in Scotland' (Bennie et al. 1997: 106). A larger proportion of objectively middle-class voters identified with the working-class and voted Labour than south of the border. Crudely expressed, it was as if an old Scotland continued to live on in the minds of the Scottish electorate. That pattern has altered since devolution, especially in the context of Holyrood elections. Paradoxically, the distinctive form of politics pre-devolution appeared to act as a break on de-alignment in Scotland but, since devolution, appears to have accelerated de-alignment. But what made Scottish politics distinct was not simply the existence of the SNP.

New Labour was in part a response to the decline of the working-class after 1945, a need to build a coalition of support that extended beyond its declining core. As Heath and MacDonald (1987) noted, social change between 1964 and 1988 cost Labour about 5 per cent of its 'natural' support raising questions as to whether there was room for class politics or socialism in Labour's programme (Heath et al. 2001: 18–29). However, while class de-alignment may have occurred across Britain (Crewe, Sarlvik and Alt 1977), this thesis was felt to be insufficiently attentive to the 'contextualised meaning of social class in political action' in different parts of Britain (Brown et al. 1996: 142). Labour's dominance of Scottish politics pre-devolution was also based on an efficient vote within a favourable electoral system. Labour's overall share of the vote in Scotland reached its high point in 1966 when it won 49.9 per cent of the vote and 64.8 per cent of Scottish seats, but its highest share of seats came in 1997 when it won 77.8 per cent of Scottish seats with only 45.6 per cent of the vote. The electoral system had created increasingly disproportional results with Labour the beneficiary.

These pictures today are very different from those of the past, not least because society has changed. It would be difficult to find many people who conform to the image conjured up by the 'working-class' in previous decades. The decline of Scottish heavy industries, the changing nature of employment, the reduction in the number of council houses and the decline of trade union membership has altered Scottish society and Scottish electoral politics.

It has now become standard practice to consider the national identities of voters in Scottish elections. This follows the work of Juan Linz, who pioneered the question often referred to in the UK as the 'Moreno Question' (for origins see Peres 2007).[2] We might have expected two related phenomena had the centre-periphery cleavage been in the process of supplanting other cleavages in determining electoral behaviour. First, there would have been an increase in the proportions of people inclined to identify towards the Scottish end of the political spectrum than in the past and secondly that the SNP's opponents would have dominated the 'British not Scottish' end of the spectrum. However, the picture is far less clear. There has not been a statistically significant increase in identification with the Scottish end of the spectrum since 2007. The SNP has increased its support across the entire spectrum but especially among the small group who see themselves as exclusively British. Perhaps most counterintuitive is the fact that the SNP won as much support as the Conservatives, traditionally seen as the quintessentially British party, among those who saw themselves as 'British not Scottish'. Once more, as Table 2.4 shows, the SNP picked up support in parts of the electorate previously thought beyond its reach and could claim to be as attractive to British identifiers as its competitors.

An alternative explanation for changing electoral behaviour focused on changing values. Old class alignments based on materialism were thought to have been replaced by post-material values (Flanagan 1987; Inglehart 1999). In his early work on post-materialist politics, Inglehart had included study of ethno-regionalist parties and suggested that some support for some of these parties was linked to a form of post-material identity politics (Inglehart 1977). However, support for the SNP has been materialist rather than post-materialist in the past (Bennie et al. 1997: 106–7). Given the backdrop of economic insecurity and imminent public spending cuts, we might expect that materialist concerns in some form would dominate the

Table 2.4 List vote by national identity, 2011 (changes since 2007)

	Scottish not British	More Scottish than British	Equally Scottish and British	More British than Scottish	British not Scottish	Other
Conservative	3 (–)	7 (–1)	22 (+3)	22 (+3)	22 (–11)	20 (–6)
Labour	17 (–4)	28 (–3)	33 (–6)	28 (–11)	35 (–3)	23 (+8)
Lib Dem	3 (–2)	4 (–6)	6 (–8)	14 (–)	7 (–4)	6 (–4)
SNP	66 (+6)	49 (+15)	29 (+13)	22 (+6)	24 (+18)	31 (+13)
Others	11 (–)	12 (–5)	10 (+7)	14 (+1)	11 (–1)	20 (–11)
	N = 366	N = 400	N = 387	N = 59	N = 129	N = 72

Scottish elections. The proportion of people citing the economy and unemployment increased considerably compared with 2007 with around 45 per cent of our survey mentioning these as the most important issue in Scotland. It would appear that 2011 was a classic materialist election. The SNP's success had little to do with post-materialism or the rise of identity politics.

A base model of the 2011 Scottish Parliament vote

In this section we introduce our 'base' model predicting the 2011 Holyrood vote. We will begin with the caveat that this is not our 'fully specified' model of the vote – it is the model that assesses the independent effects of our swathe of socio-economic and demographic variables on the vote, establishing the beginning of the causal chain or 'funnel of causality' (Campbell et al. 1960) helping us to evaluate the predictors of individual voting behaviour in the Scottish elections. Readers wishing to know 'who dunnit' before reading all of the clues and facts can skip ahead to Chapter 6 for our fully specified and kitted out multi-variate model of voting behaviour. For now, we wish to examine the relative, independent utility of the socio-demographic concepts considered in this chapter. As we build the argument of the book, we will also build out this model.

Given the multi-party system that has developed in Scotland, modelling the vote is a bit more complicated than it is in a simple two-party system such as the United States. There, one simple logistic regression model is all that is needed to examine the factors that push or pull voters toward one party or the other. In Scotland, voters have a far greater number of parties to consider on election day – and that means that the variable indicating which party a voter selected is a 'categorical' variable, indicating a series of discrete choices that do not have an inherent ordering.[3] Thus, the models that we run to predict the vote in this book are a bit more involved than the basic logistic models that are often used to model vote choice (Johns et al. 2009). Here we decided to model as fully as possible the Scottish vote, and not limit ourselves to a series of independent comparisons through logistic models comparing, say, the Labour vs. SNP vote. To include the other parties in the model, we use multinomial logistic regression to model the 2011 vote. This technique, while sounding complicated, is conceptually straightforward. Multinomial logistic models use a series of independent predictor variables to determine the odds, or probability of each possible outcome of the dependent variable – in this case vote choice. Thus, using these models, we can begin to better understand what are the statistically (and substantively) significant traits, attitudes and dispositions of individuals that predict their vote choice. As we 'build' toward our final vote choice model in Chapter 6, we will add to the list of predictor variables, examining to see which attitudes and predispositions individuals hold help us better understand voting behaviour in Scottish elections.

As we indicated with our caveat above, however, in this section we have a more modest goal. Here we seek to examine the socioeconomic and demographic factors that might help us predict an individual's vote choice. It is important to develop this basic understanding using multi-variate modelling techniques, because it is through these statistical models that we begin to understand the extent to which individual traits or characteristics have an independent effect on vote choice once we control for the other relevant traits and characteristics. For example, it might seem that, say, whether someone lives in an urban or rural area is a strong predictor of the way they vote when we look at the basic tabulations; however, once we control for other factors such as social class and trade union membership we find out that it is those variables that are actually the relevant considerations and that where the individual lives really does not matter after all.

In the results we present below, in addition to the standard sociodemographic factors, such as age, sex, education, social class, religion, employment sector (private versus public), trade union membership and urban (vs. rural) residence, we opted to also include newspaper readership (tabloid versus non-reader and broadsheet versus non-reader).

In these initial models, we broke down each of the predictor variables into a series of discrete indicator (dummy) variables to assist in understanding how the individual subgroups voted in 2011. As multinomial logistic regressions create a rather substantial volume of statistical output, the full statistical models are presented in Appendix 2. In the chapters, we will adopt the convention of presenting the changes in predicted probabilities derived from the models. These statistics tell us the extent to which a variable increases (or decreases) the probability that a voter will have opted to vote for one party rather than the others.

Figure 2.1 presents the model predicting the regional, or list, vote based on our set of socio-demographic predictors. Before discussing the more interesting findings, we should first offer a brief point on why we present models of the list vote (and not the constituency vote). In Scotland's mixed-member proportional electoral system (discussed in greater detail below) voters, of course, cast two ballots – one for a 'constituency MSP' who is selected using the basic single-member district, plurality system and one for a party's 'list' of candidates who are selected using a closed-list proportional system. All of the major parties contest all of the regional list contests, but in 2011 only the SNP and Labour contested all of the constituency contests. This means that in many constituencies in Scotland, voters simply did not have the option to vote for the Liberal Democrats or even the Conservatives. Thus the list contests provide us with a somewhat 'cleaner' assessment of what drives individuals to select one party over the other as all of the major parties contested all of the regional list contests and all voters were then able to choose between the parties.

Overall, the socio-demographic variable model leaves a good deal of room for improvement in our modelling exercises in the chapters that follow (Pseudo-R² = 0.06). That is, the socio-demographic variables alone are not terribly strong predictors of vote choice in Scotland. A casual glance down the predicted probabilities shows that few of the variables help beyond a 5 per cent increase in the predicted probability of selecting one of the parties. Further, given the

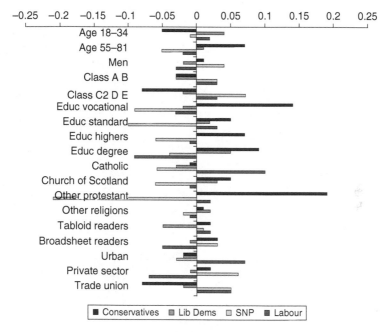

Figure 2.1 Multinomial logistic regression of list vote on socio-demographic predictors

somewhat anaemic results, it will not be surprising to most readers that very few of the variables are statistically significant in predicting one party vote versus another. For example, the *only* variable that improves our chances of predicting whether someone voted SNP vs. Labour (controlling for all of the other variables in the model) is whether or not the person is employed in the private sector (versus the public sector) – being a private sector employee increased the probability of voting SNP by about 6 per cent. This simple finding clearly supports the point made above – it is now very difficult to easily distinguish between Labour and SNP voters using the classic socio-demographic predictors. They just simply do not provide any statistically significant leverage in improving our prediction about how someone is likely to vote.

Looking at the rest of the variables and comparisons, it should not be a surprise to find that people classified as 'Other Protestant' – these largely being Anglicans – are far more likely to vote Conservative (and much less likely to vote SNP). People whose profession places them in the 'working class' and trade union members are still significantly more likely to vote Labour (and significantly less likely to vote Conservative). And people with university degrees are more likely to vote Liberal Democrat while tabloid readers tend to shun them.

What if we include the other variable mentioned above, national identity? How do responses to the 'Moreno question' stack up compared to social class and the other socio-demographic variables? In short, national identity dwarfs the other variables in the model. Controlling for the other variables in the model, people who identify as 'Scottish not British' are about 60 per cent more likely to vote SNP compared to people who identify as 'British not Scottish'. On the other hand, the probability of people at the far end of the British side of the scale is about 30 per cent higher than people at the far Scottish side.

With voters seeming to be increasingly comfortable with the idea of shifting their vote between parties come election day, it is becoming an increasingly difficult task to identify the 'typical' voter based on social and demographic traits alone. Indeed, as we have pointed out here, the only 'social' trait that distinguished between a Labour and SNP voter – once we put them all in the same model and controlled for the effects of the other social traits – was whether the voter was employed in the private or public sector. Therefore, as we will show in later chapters, we need to take into account other factors to model vote choice in the 2011 election.

Electoral system effects

Labour's dominance of Scottish electoral politics in the late twentieth century was assisted by an electoral system that favoured the party. The disproportionate effects of the system became increasingly evident with the erosion of Labour support. While Labour lost votes, it held onto its seats. The system was highly disproportional (see Figure 2.2) though not on the scale that existed in Wales where Labour's advantage was even greater than it was in Scotland (Jones and Scully 2008). This fed into debates on the nature of devolution in the 1980s and 1990s when a consensus was reached among supporters of a Scottish Parliament that an alternative, more proportionate, system ought to be introduced.

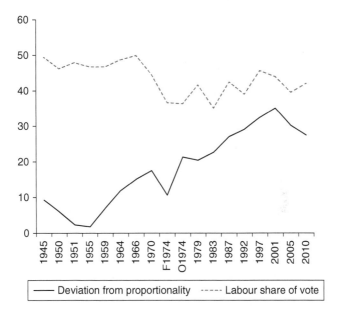

Figure 2.2 Deviation from proportionality and Scottish Labour's share of the vote, 1945–2010 UK elections

There are competing perspectives on the reasons that the MMP electoral system was adopted for elections to the Scottish Parliament. An idealist perspective was offered by Brown who argued that devolution's architects wanted to

> usher in a way of politics that is radically different from the rituals of Westminster; more participative, more creative, less confrontational [...] a culture of openness which will enable the people to see how decisions are being taken in their name, and why. The Parliament we propose is much more than a mere institutional adjustment.
>
> (Brown 2000: 542)

The more rationalist explanation acknowledges party interests. While Labour would lose out under MMP and have less chance to have an overall majority, it needed to concede this in order to win cross-party

Table 2.5   Constituency list share of the vote by party

	SNP	Labour	Conservatives	Liberal democrats
1999	1.7	5.0	0.2	1.7
2003	2.9	5.2	1.0	3.5
2007	1.9	3.0	2.7	4.5
2011	1.4	5.4	1.5	2.7

support for devolution but also created what was expected to be a break on the SNP achieving an overall majority (Table 2.5). The expectation had been that no party would be able to achieve an overall majority was understandable. In Wales, where a less proportional form of MMP was introduced for devolution at the same time, Rhodri Morgan, Welsh First Minister in 2000–2009, explained that the Welsh system had been devised to ensure that Labour would win an overall majority in three out of four elections (Osmond 2005: 7). In fact, no party has yet succeeded in winning an overall majority in Wales though Welsh Labour won 30 of the Assembly's 60 seats in 2011 when the SNP achieved an overall majority in the Scottish Parliament. The SNP won 53 constituency seats in 2011 on 45.4 per cent of the vote, the same number of constituencies Labour had won in 1999 on 38.8 per cent of the vote showing that the simple plurality element of MMP in Scotland still favoured Labour. As Table 2.5 shows, the SNP managed to retain a higher proportion of its constituency to list vote than Labour. Over four elections, the difference between Labour's constituency and list share of the vote has been between 3.0 and 5.4 per cent while the SNP's has been between 1.4 and 2.9 per cent. Labour's 1999 list vote was 5 per cent less than its efficient constituency vote resulting in it winning only 3 of the 56 list seats. By contrast, the SNP's list vote in 2011 was only 1.4 per cent less than its high constituency vote giving the SNP 16 list seats and an overall majority whereas Labour won only 3 list seats (Figure 2.3).

Scottish Labour's advantage under the simple plurality electoral system used for Westminster elections has been increasingly compromised under each successive MMP, Scottish Parliament election. The party's share of the constituency vote has fallen at each election under devolution but its share of the list vote has offered little by way of compensation. Put another way, for Labour to have maintained

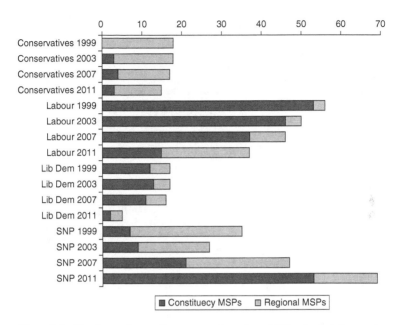

Figure 2.3 Number of constituency and region MSPs elected by party, 1999–2011

(or advanced) its share of seats in the Scottish Parliament, it would have needed to adopt a strategy seeking more list seats to offset losses in constituencies – a strategy it has been unable to implement successfully. On the other hand, the SNP had long been the main loser under the single-member constituency, simple plurality electoral system used for the general (UK) elections (though in Scotland the Conservatives have since overtaken them in this respect) but, as Figure 2.3 shows, have been the clear winners under Scotland's MMP system. However, the electoral system alone does not explain the SNP's advance.

Flows of the vote

Aggregate data shows that the SNP's support rose in 2011 compared with 2007, having fallen back in the UK general election in 2010. It also shows that the Liberal Democrat vote collapsed in 2011 while votes for the Conservatives and Labour declined between 2007 and

2011. It would be tempting to assume that the SNP advance simply involved former Liberal Democrat voters shifting *en masse* to the SNP in 2011. The SES data allows us to look below the surface of the aggregate data and observe flows of vote. This disproves pre-election predictions that Liberal Democrat decline would mainly be to Labour's advantage but also some media commentators' immediate post-election assertions that former Liberal Democrat voters moved as an undifferentiated mass to the SNP. While the SNP was the main beneficiary of the Liberal Democrat decline, there were important flows of voters between the SNP and Labour over the four years between the 2007 and 2011 elections. There are two ways of ascertaining where the increased support for the SNP came from: responses to questions asking voters to recall how they had voted in previous elections and observing how the same voters, who are part of a long-term panel of respondents, voted over time. Our data allows us to consider both.

What becomes clear from the panel data displayed in Table 2.6, which compares the same SES respondents' the reported vote in 2007 and 2011, is that the SNP was particularly successful in retaining the support of those who had voted SNP in constituency contests in 2007. The collapse of the Liberal Democrats resulted in the party retaining only a third of those who had voted for it in 2007 with the SNP winning a slightly higher proportion. But the SNP also won the support of one in five of those who had voted Labour in 2007 and one in ten of previous Conservative voters. Labour's loss of support to the SNP was partly offset by winning a similar proportion of former Conservative voters as had the SNP and 16 per cent of former Liberal Democrat voters. A similar pattern occurred with the list vote but the pattern is slightly more complicated by the fact that the Greens and others contested lists and not constituencies. The Greens succeeded in winning over the same proportion of former Labour voters from 2007 as the SNP, but once more the SNP was the main beneficiary across the board picking up far more support than it lost.

There had, of course, been a UK general election between the 2007 and 2011 Scottish parliamentary elections at which Scottish Labour performed particularly strongly. In 2010, Labour had increased its share of the vote by 2.5 percentage points to 42 per cent making it indisputably Scotland's largest Westminster party with over twice as many votes as the SNP, its nearest rival. Only managing to hold on to

Table 2.6 Vote in 2011 (constituency and region) by 2007 vote for the panel respondents

Constituency		Panel 2007 vote				Other
2011 vote	Did not vote	Con	Lab	LD	SNP	
Did not vote	41	2	10	7	3	2.94
Conservative	9	61	5	4	1	15
Labour	16	10	61	16	6	9
Lib Dem	4	7	4	33	3	9
SNP	24	11	19	37	84	41
Other	6	8	1	3	3	24
N	82	88	97	73	210	34

Region		Panel 2007 vote				Green	Other
2011 vote	Did not vote	Con	Lab	LD	SNP		
Did not vote	42	3	12	6	4	3	3
Conservative	11	71	3	11	4	0	8
Labour	13	4	60	27	3	10	11
Lib Dem	1	3	4	25	2	7	8
SNP	21	9	10	21	79	20	27
Green	2	1	11	6	2	47	8
Other	10	9	1	6	8	13	36
N	82	76	74	53	194	75	30

a much smaller core of Nationalist voters, the SNP struggles to attain the levels of support in elections to the Commons that it achieves in Holyrood elections and so it is little surprise to find that almost nine in ten of those who had voted SNP at the previous year's UK election voted for that party in 2011. The Scottish Liberal Democrats had become Scotland's second party in share of the Commons vote in 2005, outpolling the SNP by almost 5 per cent though the SNP pulled slightly ahead of the Liberal Democrats in 2010. In the 2011 Scottish election, the SNP took more than one in five of those who had voted for the Conservatives at the previous year's UK general election, almost four in ten of those who had voted Liberal Democrat

Table 2.7   Constituency vote in 2011 by recalled 2010 general election vote

Constituency		Recalled 2010 general election vote				Other
2011 vote	Did not vote	Con	Lab	LD	SNP	
Did not vote	70	6	13	12	6	26
Conservative	2	59	1	2	1	7
Labour	11	6	59	17	2	10
Lib Dem	1	5	2	28	0	7
SNP	14	21	25	38	88	30
Other	2	3	1	4	2	19
N	149	241	502	272	425	174

and one in four of those who had voted Labour (see Table 2.7). Though the UK general election was held only a year earlier, voters were even more inclined to alter their behaviour between this and the 2011 Scottish election than over the longer period between the Holyrood elections. In Chapter 5 we return to this issue with an examination of how voters' partisan allegiances shift as they compare the UK and Scottish political systems.

Conclusion

Using socio-demographic variables alone, it is difficult to paint a picture of typical SNP voters in 2011 that distinguishes them from Labour voters. The SNP has become a catch-all party (Kirchheimer 1966). For a party that styles itself 'National', this might seem easy as this suggests an appeal to all socio-demographic groups and a rejection of a special appeal to sectional groups. Yet the SNP's 'National' refers to Scotland, not the state as a whole, so this might be expected to have limited its appeal, as indeed had been the case in the past. But this was not the case in 2011. What emerges from this chapter is the clear finding that the SNP's appeal across all social groups, especially among groups where it had previously done relatively poorly. Recall that the rising tide of support for the SNP in 2011 raised their support across all socio-demographic groups.

There is also little doubt that the electoral system has worked to the SNP's advantage (or the SNP has worked the electoral system to its advantage) but even this does not explain why the SNP succeeded in winning an overall majority. This comes down to the simple explanation: the SNP succeeded not only in doing well on the simple plurality element but succeeded in winning a similarly high proportion of list voters. In sum, the SNP's ability to retain its support – from 2007 to 2011 and from constituency vote to list vote – combined with winning the lion's share of defecting former Liberal Democrat voters provided it with an overall majority. This may mean that there is no typical SNP voter but it also indicates the emergence of a very different party system from that of the recent past. While we have outlined *who* voted for the main parties in this chapter, we will consider *why* they did so in subsequent chapters.

3

Parties and Leaders

Although the Scottish Parliament has often been presented as a form of 'new politics', it is essentially a Westminster-style Parliament (Mitchell 2010b). Its electoral system is its most obvious distinguishing feature but in terms of the classic functions of parliaments (Copeland and Patterson 1994: 154), Holyrood is part of the Westminster family. This is evident in its linkage function, the relationship between the electorate and the government – in choosing the legislative branch, Scottish voters also (indirectly) choose the executive branch.

Voters' attitudes to the contending parties are therefore crucial. Indeed, while all of the chapters in this book are, in some way, shape or form, concerned with voters' attitudes to parties – to the social groups that they defend, to their policies and broader ideologies, to their records in office, to their relationships with Westminster – the particular focus of this chapter is on voters' impressions of the parties themselves. Do voters feel allegiance to one of the competing parties and, if so, does that loyalty translate into a vote for that party? Do they at least like some parties more than other parties, and what does the pattern of likes and dislikes tell us about the nature of party competition in Scotland? What images do the parties project to the electorate? Which – if any (amid general public scepticism about politics) – are seen as trustworthy or positive, or in touch with ordinary Scots?

Voters' impressions of a party are often affected by their impressions of its leader. Butler and Stokes highlighted the importance of party leaders in British elections (Butler and Stokes 1974: ch.17).

This is particularly relevant in a system of government in which the executive is chosen from within the legislature and electoral competition is often presented as a competition to become chief executive between different party leaders. It has become customary within the Westminster system for the leader of the largest party to form the government. In strict constitutional terms, as is the case in practice in many multi-party polities in which no single party dominates, this need not be the case. Indeed, Gordon Brown as leader of the Labour Party sought to hang on to office as Prime Minister despite his party coming second to the Conservatives after the 2010 UK general election. Nonetheless, the general expectation as expressed in media commentary was that the leader of the largest party would form the government. The Scottish Parliament's electoral system created opportunities for a break with the British tradition; however, to date it has proved no less British than Westminster in that the leader of the largest party is assumed to have the right to become First Minister.

Holyrood does break with Westminster's tradition through an electoral system (described in Chapter 1) that dramatically increases the likelihood that the largest party in the parliament will not secure a majority of seats, resulting in coalition and even minority governments. Under successive Labour-Liberal Democrat coalition governments between 1999 and 2007, Labour, the larger party in both sessions, held the office of First Minister with the Liberal Democrats having the post of Deputy First Minister as the junior partner. From 2007 to 2011, Alex Salmond's position within his party as First Minister leading a minority government (Mitchell et al. 2012: 46–49), combined with media coverage that portrayed the SNP leader as presidential, may have enhanced the importance of 'leadership' in the 2011 election.

A leader perceived to be capable and honest helps convey an image of his or her party sharing those characteristics. Strictly speaking, the electoral choice is between constituency candidates or party lists; however, given their roles in electioneering and as potential chief executives, in modern politics party leaders have become the focus of choice themselves. This may be actively encouraged by the parties: in 2007 and again in 2011, the SNP appeared on the list ballot paper in each region as 'SCOTTISH NATIONAL PARTY Alex Salmond for First Minister'. Each of the main parties arrange media events with 'photo-opportunities', alerting the media to where the leader will be each day of the campaign. This can work against a party leader, as in the case of Iain Gray's encounter with anti-public spending cuts protesters early in the campaign. Television, however, has long been the main campaign battleground and has equally long been accused of personalizing – or 'presidentialising' – elections (Foley 1993; Mughan 2000). This tendency is exacerbated by the introduction of leader debates. Of course, leadership debates were a feature of Scottish Parliamentary elections prior to the Westminster leaders' debates in 2010. Televised Scottish debates were standard in by-elections in Scotland prior to devolution with the format adopted and then largely replicated for the leadership contests since devolution. Nonetheless, despite this focus on the party leaders, there remains disagreement among students of politics of the importance of leaders in electoral contests. Research on British general elections and elections in other European polities concluded that there was little evidence to corroborate widespread media and public perceptions that the personalities of leaders influenced elections (Bartle and Crewe 2002; Curtice and Holmberg 2005).

Leaders can be victims of their parties as well as vice versa. A popular leader will not drag a deeply unpopular party to victory; in any case, it is hard to be a popular leader of an unpopular party because the negative image tends to rub off. There are complex reciprocal relations between the public images of parties and their leaders, with the two often inextricably entangled in voters' minds (Butt 2006). What is clear is that leaders have the *potential* to win votes both as individuals and as shapers of their party's image. We need therefore to examine voters' evaluations of both leaders and parties, and it also makes sense to do so in the same chapter.

Party identification

Party identification is the starting point for any analysis of voters' attitudes towards parties. At its most basic, party identification, or partisanship, reflects the fact that voters do not approach the parties afresh at each election. Most people have inclinations, sometimes of very long standing, towards a certain party and often against others. Understanding electoral behaviour in 2011 requires that we take account of the various ways in which voters were predisposed towards or against different choices. This matters not only because party identifiers are highly likely to vote for the party to which they have an enduring attachment. Partisanship also acts as a 'perceptual screen' through which identifiers view politics (Campbell et al. 1960; Zaller 1992). For example, those who support a party are more likely to view that party's leader favourably, more likely to take a dim view of its opponents' economic competence and less likely to support a policy proposed by another party. Thus, party identification can have both a direct effect and an indirect effect on vote choice. Even if identifiers do not choose *their* party simply out of habit, they are likely to do so because their interpretation of political events, issues and personalities steer them in that direction. The second point means that partisanship remains an important consideration in later chapters of this book. For now, we simply assess the partisan profile of the Scottish electorate going into the 2011 contest.

Before looking at the survey evidence, we recall the disagreement on the nature and origins of party identification. The 'traditional' or Michigan interpretation (so called because it was developed by Angus Campbell and his colleagues from the University of Michigan), suggested that partisanship is an emotional bond with a particular party, not unlike religious, national or sporting identities (Campbell et al. 1960; Green et al. 2002). Like these, it is typically acquired early from parents and tends to endure, and often strengthen, over a voter's lifetime (Butler and Stokes 1974; Tilley 2003). This account goes a long way to explain why quite a large fraction of the electorate turns out and votes for the same party in election after election. It can also explain the inter-generational transmission of partisanship. Some families have supported the same party for many decades, which, in turn, explains why the menu of parties available to voters can change little over long periods. A different account of partisanship was presented by Fiorina (1981) and has been adopted in the British context by Clarke et al. (2004, ch. 6; see also Clarke and McCutcheon 2009). On the 'revisionist' or Fiorina account, party identification is not seen as an emotional tie or loyalty to a particular party but as little more than attitudes towards the political parties much the same as people view party leaders, television shows and work colleagues. These attitudes represent 'running tallies' of their assessments, whether positive or negative, of the parties over time. Such assessments may be based on the usual wide range of factors – leaders, policies, priorities, record in office, and so on – and the detailed information is often forgotten. But the overall tallies remain and, for Fiorina, they represent party identification: that is, voters' predispositions to vote for or against a party at any given election.

This revisionist approach has two major explanatory strengths. First, survey evidence has long documented a marked fall in the proportion of voters reporting the kind of strong party identification described by the Michigan model. The reasons are in some dispute but the trend, known as partisan de-alignment, is unmistakable in virtually all Western democracies (Dalton and Wattenberg 2000). The proportion of voters describing themselves as 'very strong' or 'fairly strong' identifiers has declined from around three-quarters to around half of the Scottish electorate (Johns et al. 2010: 41–44). That leaves a half of the electorate whose partisan predispositions are better captured by Fiorina's dynamic attitudinal model than by the kind of enduring emotional identity envisaged in the Michigan model. The second advantage of the Fiorina model is that it explains why, as revealed by panel surveys, party identification at the individual level is less stable than is consistent with a lifetime-loyalty model.

Any debate about which account of partisanship is 'correct' tends to obscure what would otherwise be an obvious point: both models may be correct but for different parts of the electorate. Recent analyses suggest instead a 'mover-stayer' model, whereby some partisans maintain their allegiances but plenty of others withdraw their support or even transfer it to a different party. These switches can be explained by exactly those factors – events, performance, changes of leadership and so on – that Fiorina identified as driving voters' running tallies. The reason why the distinction matters here is because of the changing patterns of party competition in Scotland. Over 90 per cent of voters supported either Labour or the Conservatives in every election between 1950 and 1959, and between 80 and 90 per cent from 1964 to 1970. These parties had deep social roots, identification with which was passed down through the generations, while few voters supported the Liberals and only tiny fractions of the Scottish electorate declared any attachment to the then fringe SNP. Since 1970, however, the combined Labour and Conservative vote has not exceeded 70 per cent except in 1979 when together they won 72.9 per cent of the vote. De-alignment has weakened but not eradicated the process of inter-generational transmission of partisanship, and so the long-established Labour and Conservative parties can still call upon at least some traditional loyalists – particularly among older voters. The SNP's support may also reflect a mix of 'movers' and 'stayers'. On the one hand, SNP support may reflect Fiorina-style identification: that is, voters are predisposed to the party because their accumulated experience of its policies, image, leadership and record; however, the SNP too may have developed an inter-generational Michigan type of party identifiers since its electoral breakthrough in the late 1960s.

Given that a large and growing proportion of the Scottish electorate has no strong partisan allegiance, we use the familiar two-part question to measure party identification. In the pre-election survey, respondents were first asked whether they thought of themselves as a supporter of any one political party, to which 56 per cent of respondents answered 'yes', up from 50 per cent in 2007. There was also an increase in the proportion of 'leaners', respondents who answered 'no' to the question above but 'yes' to whether they thought of themselves as a 'little closer to one political party than to the others'. In 2011, leaners comprised 28 per cent of the Scottish electorate, leaving just 16 per cent who answered 'no' to both questions, disclaiming either identification or leaning. The corresponding percentages in 2007 were 24 per cent and 26 per cent, so leaners have gone from being outnumbered by non-identifiers to clearly outnumbering them. These changes are statistically significant and interrupt what had been assumed to be an inexorable trend of de-alignment. Something about the 2011 election appears to have 'activated' some partisan leanings that had lain dormant for a while, as we will discuss below.

Respondents answering 'yes' to either of the questions above are then asked to name the party. The distribution of identification and leaning among the parties, in both 2011 and 2007, is shown in Table 3.1. Looking first at the identifiers, that is those declaring support for one of the parties, the proportion of those identifying as Labour and SNP are almost a mirror image of these parties' share of the vote – but with the Labour and the SNP percentages reversed. So the 2011 outcome was anything but a simple reflection of the parties' core strengths in the electorate. In fact, as predicted earlier, Labour enjoys a large advantage over the Nationalists in terms of 'traditional' partisanship. This advantage was wider in 2011 than 2007,

Table 3.1 Partisanship (identification, leaning and combined) in 2007 and 2011

	Identifiers		Leaners		Combined	
	2011	2007	2011	2007	2011	2007
Conservative	16	16	14	17	12	12
Labour	46	40	33	30	35	27
Lib Dem	8	10	8	15	7	9
SNP	28	30	34	27	25	21
Others	2	5	11	11	4	5
None	–	–	–	–	16	26
N	1,141	874	574	414	2,046	1,774

Source: Pre-election survey.

again at odds with the election results. The explanation may lie in the changing political context, notably the change of government at Westminster. As discussed in Chapter 1, Labour performed well in the 2010 general election in Scotland and in subsequent opinion polls. The return of a Conservative-led government at Westminster may have refreshed Labour sympathies that had faded in recent years.

That may explain Labour's strengthened advantage in terms of 'core vote'. It leaves unanswered the question of why this did not translate into victory but heavy defeat in the Scottish Parliament election. Two points about the role of party identification in 2011 are notable. The first is a reminder that there is more to partisanship than the Michigan-style loyalties that are thought to be measured by the party identification question. We simply cannot equate 'identifiers' with Michigan partisans and 'leaners' with Fiorina partisans, though conceptually a partisan leaning, that is, not explicitly identifying with a party but inclining towards one, would seem to be better captured by the Fiorina explanation of voting behaviour. It is notable that the Labour-SNP gap closed completely among the leaners in 2011. The SNP may have fewer loyalists but has as many sympathizers as Labour and its share of leaners grew appreciably compared with 2007.

Nonetheless, as the final column, combining identifiers and leaners, in Table 3.1 shows, Labour went into the 2011 election with a significant advantage over the SNP, and an even wider margin over all

Table 3.2 Pre-election party identification and regional vote

Regional vote	Pre-election party identification				
	Con %	Lab %	LD %	SNP %	None %
Conservative	**73**	0	2	1	6
Labour	1	**66**	5	0	13
Lib Dem	1	1	**45**	0	4
SNP	12	9	19	**85**	34
Other	3	7	16	5	16
Did not vote	11	16	13	8	27
N	150	449	86	276	762

Sources: Pre- and post-election surveys (weighted by turnout).

of the other parties, in terms of partisan predispositions. The second key point about party identification, and another step in explaining the election outcome, is that the SNP was markedly better than Labour at mobilizing those predisposed to support the party. Table 3.2 shows the voting behaviour (regional vote) of those who reported identifying with – that is, not just leaning towards – one of the parties and, in the final column, of those disclaiming any identification. Unsurprisingly, the Liberal Democrats had by far the greatest difficulty in retaining their identifiers: less than half (45 per cent) of their much-reduced support base voted for the party. The corresponding proportion for Labour is around two-thirds (66 per cent), a long way adrift of the 85 per cent retention achieved by the SNP. Not only were Labour identifiers the likeliest to abstain (16 per cent) but a non-trivial proportion (9 per cent) actually voted for the party's main rival for government. By contrast, while a few self-reported SNP identifiers took advantage of the regional vote to choose a small 'Other' party, virtually none defected to any of its major rivals.

The SNP's success, therefore, went beyond mobilizing and retaining its own support. The party also won over partisans from across the spectrum (12 per cent of Conservatives and 19 per cent of Liberal Democrats), as well as proving far the most popular party among the large group of non-identifiers. Supporters of all the other three major parties were more likely to defect to the SNP than to any other party. There is an echo here of the results in Chapter 2, which also showed the Nationalists winning support across the demographic board rather than from some particular part of the community. The same was true in 2007 and indeed these results closely parallel those from an equivalent analysis at that election (Johns et al. 2010: 43). The SNP maintained its progress while Labour continued to struggle. There are two reasons for the disparity between Labour and the SNP in the ease with which they converted predispositions into votes. The first is simple. Electoral behaviour is a function both of long-term loyalties and short-term factors and, as is clear from comparing Table 3.1 with the election results, the SNP had a considerable advantage in terms of short-term factors. As the Fiorina model highlights, party identifiers may be resistant, but are not impervious, to those short-term factors. The second point is less obvious and more speculative. It is exemplified by our suggestion that developments at the UK level explain the increase or 'reactivation' of Labour identification. The party identification question begins with 'Generally speaking [...]' and is expressly intended to measure a general and enduring identity. There is no contextual cue in the question and no mention of the upcoming election. However, survey respondents answer questions with the considerations that are uppermost in their mind at the time, and the multi-level nature of the Scottish polity means that these considerations could derive from different contexts. In particular, it is conceivable that those reporting a Labour attachment tend to have Westminster politics in mind, while SNP identification is more common among those thinking about the Scottish context in which that party is relatively strong and, more recently, also in power. If that is the case, then it is not hard to see why Labour identifiers were more prone to abstain or to defect in 2011, because their identification is rooted in a different electoral sphere. Put another way, Labour identities were not activated by the 2011 election as they had been the previous year. This is a speculative argument because to date there has been no test of the hypothesis that citizens' party identifications might be specific to a level of government. However, in Chapter 5, which is all about placing the 2011 election in its multi-level context, we provide just such a test.

For now, we recap the discussion so far. Labour went into the 2011 election, as it has in all previous Scottish Parliament contests, with a clear advantage in terms of partisan attachments. Yet the party was unable to capitalize on this historical legacy. As far as Labour and, especially, the Liberal Democrats were concerned, party identification did not mean party loyalty: substantial portions of what should have been the parties' 'core vote' chose another party or stayed at home. Although the decline in party identification seems to have been arrested, around half of the voters still only lean towards a party (and as often towards the SNP as towards Labour) or are, in American electoral parlance, 'independents'. For the parties, an advantage among long-term partisans needs to be accompanied by an appeal to 'floating' voters. All the signs so far are that the SNP's short-term appeal far outstripped that of Labour and the other contenders in 2011. In the next section we confirm the point.

Partisan attitudes

According to Fiorina (1981), voters maintain and update 'running tally' attitudes towards the competing parties, and electoral choice is principally a reflection of those attitudes. Put simply, voters opt for the party with the highest tally. This model was developed in the resolutely two-party US system but there is no reason why the same should not apply in Scotland's multi-party system. Here, then, we look at voters' attitudes to the parties via a simple measure, a 0–10 scale running from 'strongly dislike' to 'strongly like', that captures these running tallies. These like-dislike ratings are, of course, influenced by partisanship – the strongest Michigan-style identifiers will like their party a great deal and the others not at all – but they also reflect a range of shorter-term evaluations, recent and not so recent, although probably weighted towards the former. They thus give the clearest idea of the 'state of the parties' going in to the 2011 election.

The first column of Table 3.3 shows the mean rating of each party among all respondents in the pre-election survey (excluding those who said 'don't know' – usually small numbers except in the case of the less familiar Green Party). The 2007 ratings are provided in the next column for comparison. One notable contrast between the two elections is that the mean ratings are more dispersed in 2011. In 2007, three of the four major parties were clustered between 4.4 and 4.8. Four years later, the Liberal Democrats' popularity had fallen almost to the depths long plumbed in Scottish public opinion by the Conservatives while, perhaps less predictably, the ratings of the two leading parties had increased significantly. This apparently positive news for Labour needs to be tempered by two points. First, echoing

Table 3.3 Mean party ratings on 0–10 scale: (i) all respondents (ii) by party identification

Party rated	All respondents		2011 by party identification				
	2011	2007	Con	Lab	LD	SNP	None
Conservative	3.0	3.2	8.6	1.3	3.7	2.0	3.1
Labour	5.1	4.4	1.5	8.5	3.9	3.6	4.7
Lib Dem	3.4	4.7	5.2	2.4	7.9	2.6	3.6
SNP	5.9	4.8	3.5	4.7	4.9	9.3	5.9
Green	4.7	4.5	3.3	5.2	5.2	5.0	4.6
N (min.)	1783	1713	161	464	89	304	743

Source: Pre-election survey.

an earlier point, if this boost in popularity was driven more by the Westminster concerns that delivered the party's strong showing in the 2010 UK general election, it is at least questionable whether it would also pay off in a Holyrood context. Secondly, the SNP's rating rose further, thus doubling its advantage over Labour. A mean rating of 5.9, comfortably above the middle point of the scale, is impressive for a party without a large base of Michigan-style identifiers that can be relied on for very positive ratings, and doubly so in a multi-party context where each party generally has more opponents than supporters. The SNP clearly received at least grudging praise from some of those who did not vote for it.

This point is confirmed by the right-hand panel of Table 3.3, which shows the mean party ratings among groups of party (and non-) identifiers. The high scores on the central diagonal reflect the point that identifiers tend to like their party a lot more than the others, but there are some notable differences even here. Even Liberal Democrat identifiers were relatively unimpressed by their party in 2011, while the SNP's supporters were extremely satisfied. This helps to explain the differentials in mobilization and retention shown in Table 3.2, as does the relative popularity of the SNP across the partisan board. The Nationalists' ratings resemble those of the Greens, which is significant given that the latter tend to elicit widespread sympathy and to be many voters' second choice. The Conservatives' tolerance of the SNP is striking given their staunch opposition to independence, but perhaps most notable is that Labour identifiers gave the SNP almost a midpoint average rating, despite the fact that the two parties have been the leading rivals of Scottish politics for several years now. Most importantly of all, the SNP's rating amongst non-identifiers – the key electoral market – was as high as among the electorate as a whole, while Labour's popularity in this group dipped below the midpoint. Table 3.2 has already shown that the SNP's popularity advantage over Labour among non-partisans went on to deliver electoral benefits.

In 2007, the close contest between the two leading parties could be seen as the cancelling out of two differences: while Labour enjoyed a broader electoral base in terms of long-term attachments, the SNP had a lead in terms of short-term or 'running tally' attitudes. Four years later, the pattern is similar but with two key differences that help to explain why the SNP performed so strongly. Labour's advantage on party identification yielded only limited electoral benefits, perhaps because the renewed loyalty was to the new opposition at Westminster more than to the Scottish party competing in 2011. Meanwhile, the SNP had stretched its popularity advantage, especially among the key group of non-aligned or 'floating' voters, and more generally seems to have given quite a positive impression across the electorate. In the next section, on party images, we explore the sources of this positive impression and also look at why the other parties proved less attractive.

Party image

For Butler and Rose (1960: 17), 'a party image is nothing more than a party as it appears to the public, the picture left by its surface characteristics'. This definition is suitably broad because the content of these mental pictures may vary a good deal across voters, parties and elections. Nonetheless, impressions of the parties are often dominated by one or two associations that may persist over time and become widely shared within the electorate. These associations may be positive or negative but the latter tend to receive most attention. Parties in the electoral doldrums – Labour at UK level during the 1980s, and the Conservatives in Scotland since the Thatcher era – often conclude that a tarnished image or 'brand' is at the root of their problems (see, e.g., Quinn 2008).

In Chapter 2, we looked at the social class images of the parties and their associations with groups more generally. Another facet of party image might be a prominent stance on a core issue. If voters were to play a word-association game, the chances are that the name 'SNP' would be followed by the word 'independence'. The problem with both class and issue images is that they are inevitably exclusionary – they are the basis not only for attracting supporters but also for repelling those from a different social background or taking the opposite view on that issue. Hence the major parties, notably 'New Labour', have long downplayed social divisions and sought instead to appeal to all classes – that is, to be 'catch-all' parties (Kirchheimer 1966). This is a relatively recent phenomenon in Scottish politics. A generation ago, the SNP sought to claim Labour's traditional reputation as the party that best represented the working-class (Bennie et al. 1997). The SNP has sought to rebalance its image away from simply being a party committed to independence to one that places greater emphasis on a broader appeal and to being the party that represents Scottish interests of concern to the whole electorate, regardless of constitutional preferences.

What these examples show is the importance of what might be called the 'valence' aspects of party image. As discussed in more detail in the next chapter, valence objectives are those shared by the entire electorate (see Stokes 1963, 1992). Economic prosperity is a classic example and, again as discussed in Chapter 4, economic competence is a key valence aspect of party image. Yet the valence dimensions of image are often more general, as described by Butler and Stokes:

> [s]ome qualities of party image, such as strength or modernity or reliability, are so broad that they could be linked to almost any set of government outputs. A party may be seen as trustworthy or as bound to make a mess of things without any necessary reference to the area in which it can be trusted or in which it is bound to make a mess. Indeed, some image qualities have much more to do with 'intrinsic' values of party, which are not related to outputs of government at all [...]
>
> (Butler and Stokes 1974)

These are 'valence' aspects of party image because, just as no voter wants economic decline, no voter wants a governing party that is untrustworthy or incompetent. In the 2011 SES, we asked about five such 'intrinsic values' that could influence voters' willingness to support a party. Respondents were asked whether they see each of the four major parties as 'capable' or 'not capable of being a strong government'; as 'united' or 'divided'; as 'in touch' or 'out of touch with ordinary people'; as a party that 'keeps' or that 'breaks its promises'; and finally as 'standing up' or 'not standing up for Scotland'. A 'not sure' option was offered and was routinely chosen by around 15–20 per cent of respondents but these respondents are omitted from Table 3.4 to help clarify the patterns in party image. This table reports results first for all respondents and then for the important 'undecided' group, that is the approximately 20 per cent of the sample that answered at the midpoint or below on a pre-election scale from zero ('not at all') to ten ('absolutely') gauging how sure respondents were about the regional list vote choice.

Table 3.4 Party ratings on five facets of party image: (i) all respondents (ii) undecided voters

	All respondents (min. $N = 1,543$)			
	Con %	Lab %	LD %	SNP %
Capable of strong government	46	62	14	71
United	51	52	15	86
In touch with ordinary people	15	57	29	75
Keep their promises	20	31	9	50
Standing up for Scotland	18	56	27	95
	Undecided voters (min. $N = 240$)			
	Con	Lab	LD	SNP
Capable of strong government	47	65	18	66
United	52	44	18	87
In touch with ordinary people	13	53	32	66
Keep their promises	14	22	9	37
Standing up for Scotland	16	53	29	95

Source: Pre-election survey.

It is plain that images are coloured by a party's general popularity. The Liberal Democrats won little credit for anything whereas the SNP's ratings were strong across the board, but there is more to the picture than this. The Conservatives were fairly widely credited with competence and unity, even if dismissed on the other three criteria. While Labour's scorecard was generally quite good, the party's promises were not widely valued. There was a similar pattern for the SNP – there is a tendency for the electorate to distrust parties to keep their promises. However, the SNP's image as a party that stands up for Scotland was almost universally recognized. Above all, the SNP clearly projected the most favourable image in 2011. It led Labour by some distance, and the other parties even further, on all five criteria.

We might expect that undecided voters would be more sceptical and they were indeed a little less likely to give the SNP credit for keeping promises and being in touch with ordinary people. But the results in the lower panel are generally very similar to those for all respondents. In particular, the Nationalists retain their advantage over Labour on four of the five dimensions, and the gap only closes, without reversing, on capacity for strong government.

The fact that the different party image ratings are to some extent distinct from a party's general popularity means that these ratings may potentially have an independent impact on voting behaviour. There has been remarkably little research into the electoral effects of party image, one consequence of which is that we know little about the relative importance of the five facets of image examined above. One way of addressing this issue is to conduct a series of simple regression analyses for each party, predicting its 0–10 like-dislike rating based on the five assessments of its image. By also controlling for party identification in those regressions, we can mitigate the bias inherent in the fact that those who already support a party are likely to perceive it more favourably on all dimensions. The full results of the regressions are available in Appendix 2 Table 3.1; here, we illustrate in Figure 3.1 the coefficients for party image that are our main concern.

There is considerable variation across parties in the image criteria by which they are judged. Some of these differences are more easily explained than others. For instance, Labour and the SNP, the leading rivals for Holyrood office, are judged more than the others by the perceived capacity for strong government. The incumbent SNP

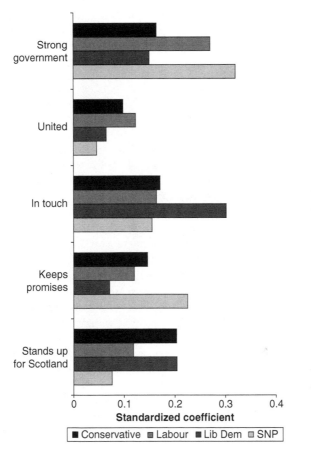

Figure 3.1 Impact (standardized regression coefficients) of image variables on party like-dislike ratings
Source: Pre-election survey.

was judged most by the worth of its promises. The Westminster governing coalition parties were judged mostly on their willingness to stand up for Scotland, though being seen as in touch with ordinary people, while somewhat important for all parties, did most to determine attitudes to the Liberal Democrats. Finally, while unity is often regarded by party elites as essential for projecting a favourable image, it matters less to voters. In order to determine what these results mean for each party, they must be read in conjunction with the ratings in Table 3.4. The broad pattern appears to be that parties are judged most on their weakest criteria. One exception is the strongest effect in all four regressions, the SNP coefficient for strong government. The Nationalists were untested as a party of government when elected in 2007; their popularity in 2011 owed a good deal to the fact that many voters saw them as having passed that test.

Another aspect that might be considered under the heading of party image is the degree to which the parties project a 'positive' image through their campaigns. In 2011 the SNP in particular seemed to be determined to appear as positive campaigners. This maintained an approach that the party adopted in 2007 and was perceived by SNP strategists as having been important in that election. Evidence from the 2007 SES supports their case. Post-election survey respondents were asked to rate each party's campaign on a five-point scale from 'very positive' to 'very negative' (with a brief description of what each entails). Not only was the SNP campaign's seen as by far the most positive and Labour's as the most negative, but these evaluations had an independent effect on party choice, even controlling for partisan predispositions and a vast array of other variables (Pattie et al., 2011; Johns et al. 2010, ch. 10).

The same questions were included in the 2011 post-election survey and the results are shown in Table 3.5. In addition to the basic percentages, we calculate a mean 'positivity' rating based on numbering the scale from one ('very negative') to five ('very positive'), and use

Table 3.5 Perceptions of campaign tone by party, 2011 and 2007

		Con %	Lab %	LD %	SNP %
Very positive		5	4	2	33
Fairly positive		24	14	16	38
Neither positive nor negative		28	19	34	16
Fairly negative		24	33	31	8
Very negative		18	30	17	4
N		1402	1434	1382	1436
Mean positivity rating	2011	2.74	2.29	2.56	3.88
(1 = v. negative, 5 = v. positive)	2007	2.97	2.29	3.09	3.30

Source: Pre-election survey.

this to provide an economical comparison with 2007. The contrast between the two leading parties is clear: as in 2007, the median respondent saw the SNP's campaign as 'fairly positive', Labour's as 'fairly negative', and the other two parties' campaigns as more mixed but on balance negative.

Labour's mean rating was unchanged across the two elections despite the fact that the focus of the party's attacks shifted between 2007 and 2011: in 2007, Labour focused its attacks on the SNP and the danger of independence while in 2011 its emphasis, particularly in the early part of the campaign, was an attempt to ride a tide of anti-Conservative feeling by trying to resurrect memories of when the Conservatives were last in government in Westminster. The Liberal Democrat mean score declined but this probably has more to do the party's tainted image as part of the coalition in London than to do with specific judgements of its 2011 Scottish campaigning. The SNP rating increased markedly, with over 71 per cent of respondents rating its campaign in one of the two 'positive' categories. That is too large a proportion to be comprised only, or even mainly, of those already predisposed towards the SNP, and the point is confirmed by looking at the campaign tone ratings of Labour identifiers. Even among that group, 63 per cent acknowledged the SNP campaign as positive but only 36 per cent said the same of their own party's campaign, 42 per cent describing the Labour approach as negative. Like other indicators of party image, perceptions of campaign tone are coloured by partisan predispositions but also contain a substantial objective component. This gives them the potential for the kind of independent impact on voting behaviour that they had in 2007. In the final chapter, we estimate the kind of full multi-variate models required to test whether the same was true this time around. For now we can conclude that, insofar as campaign tone did influence party choice in 2011, we would expect this to have worked strongly in the SNP's favour.

The leaders

Paying attention to party image raises further questions. How did voters decide whether Labour was capable of strong government, or whether the SNP would keep its promises? More broadly, what are the sources of a party's image, especially when it has been out of power for some time? One key answer to that question is the party's leader.

In introducing this chapter, we noted the 'presidentialization' processes that have placed leaders at the forefront of party and especially electoral politics. Another important point is that voters, especially those – the majority – with limited interest in and knowledge of politics, will find leaders easier to judge than parties. Voters are much more accustomed and adept at judging other humans than complex, multi-faceted and perhaps quite nebulous entities as political parties (Miller et al. 1986). When voters in 2011 were judging the SNP's performance in office, it makes sense that they would draw on their judgements of Alex Salmond, by then into his seventh year of his second stint as SNP leader, having served a full term as First Minister and very familiar on the Scottish political scene. Such inference is hardly irrational given the perceived capacity of powerful leaders to shape parties in their own image.

What we have just described would be classified by Anthony King (2002, ch. 1) as an indirect effect of leadership. Voters are choosing between parties but their view of a party, and hence their choice, is influenced by the leader's impact on that party. Leadership may also have direct effects. In that case, party is bypassed and voters simply choose between leaders – in the Scottish context, they choose among the options for First Minister. The distinction between direct and indirect effects is easily blurred because leader and party images are themselves so closely enmeshed, making it hard to say which is ultimately driving voters' choices. However, it is clear that voters' evaluations of party leaders have a significant independent impact on voting behaviour in UK general elections (Andersen and Evans 2003; Evans and Andersen 2005; Clarke et al. 2004, 2009, 2011; Stevens et al. 2011).

The evidence is a little patchier from the four Scottish elections so far. This may be due in part to a rapid turnover of leaders, which has left the average contender less familiar to voters, and in turn less influential over their choices, than was the case with major figures like Tony Blair in the 2001 and 2005 general elections, or Gordon Brown and David Cameron in 2010. But that cannot explain why, in the 2007 Scottish election, evaluations of the long-prominent Salmond had limited independent impact on party choice. This seems a case in which a leader's impact was predominantly indirect: voters liked the SNP under Salmond at least as much as they liked him personally (Johns et al. 2009). However, other analyses suggested a direct Salmond effect (Curtice et al. 2009), though this may have been a consequence of the timing of the fieldwork that took place in the period immediately following the election when the First Minister was enjoying a honeymoon effect (even among newspapers that had been, and would again be, his staunchest critics). There was also evidence that attitudes to the Labour, Conservative and Liberal Democrat leaders influenced choice in 2007 (Johns et al. 2010, ch. 10). So there is at least the potential for influence in 2011. This potential may have been reinforced by the series of televised debates between the party leaders. These did not have the novelty value of those at the UK general election a year earlier as there had been debates in previous Scottish Parliament elections. There were three leader debates, broadcast on 29 March, 1 May and 3 May, as well as a further debate between the party finance spokespeople. Between them, they reached 780,000 viewers.[1] Ratings provide a more reliable indicator of reach than do survey data like the SES results, because the kinds of politically engaged people who watch leader debates are overrepresented in survey samples like ours. So, when 33 per cent of SES respondents report that they watched at least some of one of the debates, this may overstate the proportion of viewers in the population but without implying that the survey respondents are lying.

Media reaction to each televised debate begins while the closing credits are rolling and so it is impossible, especially with a post-election survey, to gauge voters' responses to the debates themselves rather than the subsequent media narrative. We should therefore approach respondents' self-reports of debate influence with particular caution. Of those who watched the debates, 24 per cent (i.e. 8 per cent of the whole sample) said that they saw something which 'influenced their vote in the Scottish Parliament election'. Given known limits on voters' introspective capacities, that is, the fact that people seldom have a clear idea of what drives their decisions (Wilson 2004; Lodge and Taber 2013), means that we have very little idea of the accuracy of that percentage.

On the other hand, it could be that the impact of the debates is itself indirect. If voters, even those who did not watch, are repeatedly exposed to a narrative about the leaders' debating performance, with some hailed as successes and others as failures, this could influence their evaluations of those leaders and ultimately their vote

Table 3.6 Perceived best and worst debate performers: (i) all watchers (ii) by party identification

Leader	All respondents		Best, by party identification				
	Best	Worst	Con	Lab	LD	SNP	None
Anabel Goldie (Con)	14	9	49	18	15	0	18
Iain Gray (Lab)	4	68	3	18	8	0	1
Tavish Scott (Lib Dem)	1	21	5	0	15	0	1
Alex Salmond (SNP)	81	3	43	64	62	100	80
N	552	540	37	106	13	187	204

Source: Post-election survey.

choice. In that case, we can gauge public impressions of the debates as a whole, whether these impressions were first- or second-hand. Table 3.6 shows widespread public agreement on both the big winner and big loser from the debates: 76 per cent of watchers declared that Alex Salmond had done 'the best job', and 63 per cent thought that Labour's Iain Gray had done 'the worst job'. Percentages of this size cannot be explained by partisan predispositions that are distributed more evenly within the electorate. The breakdown by party identification confirms the point. While almost half of Conservative identifiers designated their leader Annabel Goldie as the winner, a clear majority within all of the other groups nominated Alex Salmond as doing the best job. In illustration of the combination of objectivity and partisan bias, all of the SNP-identifying respondents who watched the debates dutifully reported that Alex Salmond was the winner.

Although there were only two realistic contenders for First Minister in 2011, the image and popularity of each party depends in part on its leader and so attitudes to all of the Scottish leaders are important. We should extend this analysis a little further, however, to take in evaluations of the party leaders at UK level. There are theoretical and empirical reasons to suspect that the key players at Westminster had an impact on voters in 2011. As discussed in our later chapter on the multi-level context of Scottish elections (Chapter 5), those different levels are not neatly distinct but entangled and blurred. Events and personalities from one level influence choices at another level, a process encouraged by the fact that the menu of parties on offer is basically the same. We have already noted the impact of the Conservatives' return to power at Westminster; Labour's support in Scotland may have solidified in reaction to the deluge of criticism suffered by the UK party's Scottish leader, Gordon Brown. Further, UK party leaders typically participate actively in Scottish elections. David Cameron, Ed Miliband and Nick Clegg all made well-publicized stops on the 2011 campaign trail. In this context, it would not be surprising if attitudes to Westminster leaders influence Holyrood votes. Analysing party choice at the 2007 Scottish Parliament election, Johns et al. (2010: ch. 3) found that willingness to support Labour was actually influenced more by evaluations of outgoing Westminster leader Tony Blair than by those of incumbent First Minister Jack McConnell.

We measure leader evaluations with the same 0–10 like-dislike scale by which we measured feelings about parties. This does not do justice to the numerous traits and criteria against which leaders, like parties, can be judged (Stevens et al. 2011). However, previous research suggests that leadership effects can be reasonably well captured with a single affect dimension (Clarke et al. 2009), and constraints on survey space precluded a more detailed scrutiny of the various leaders' personalities. Table 3.7 reports the mean evaluation for each of the major Scottish party leaders and five potential players from Westminster. Where available, there is also a comparison with that leader's mean rating in 2007 or with the current leader's predecessor in the case of Labour and the Liberal Democrats in Scotland. There are then three further statistics for each leader: the standard deviation, which measures the spread of ratings and thus the extent to which a leader polarizes opinion; the Pearson correlation between respondents' ratings of that leader and those of his or her party, which shows the extent to which the two are separated in voters' minds; and the proportion of respondents answering 'don't know' (DK) when asked their view on that leader, indicating public familiarity with that leader.

Media treatments of the election during the campaign and especially after the results seemed to present a mismatch between the two contenders for First Minister. These pre-election ratings lend some support to that portrayal. Alex Salmond was clearly the most popular of the Scottish leaders and his advantage over Iain Gray, at 1.5

Table 3.7   Ratings of party leaders on like-dislike scale by all respondents and non-identifiers

	Mean 2011	Mean 2007	Standard deviation	Correl. with party score	% DK	N
Annabel Goldie	4.3	(4.1)	3.1	.61	16	1711
Iain Gray (Jack McConnell)	4.0	(4.0)	2.9	.68	19	1652
Tavish Scott (Nicol Stephen)	3.7	(4.3)	2.5	.55	22	1581
Alex Salmond	5.5	(4.8)	3.6	.87	9	1857
David Cameron	3.1	(3.8)	3.1	.82	6	1914
Ed Miliband	4.1	n/a	3.0	.73	9	1862
Nick Clegg	2.8	n/a	2.8	.72	7	1903
Gordon Brown	4.7	(4.4)	3.3	.75	6	1916
Tony Blair	3.5	(3.8)	3.2	.61	6	1918

Source: Pre-election survey.

points, was considerable both in absolute terms and relative to the equivalent gap in 2007 when Alex Salmond had a 0.8-point lead over Jack McConnell. It should be noted that this is not because Iain Gray was an unusually unpopular leader. His rating was no worse than Jack McConnell's had been in 2007, nor was it significantly different from 2011 evaluations of Labour's Westminster leader, Ed Miliband. On the other hand, given Labour's advantage in terms of partisan loyalties, and the boost it received from events at Westminster, Mr Gray's rating does look unimpressive. Two other statistics are telling. First, the Labour Party itself was rated fully a point higher on the like-dislike scale (see Table 3.3). Secondly, and crucially, if we look only at the ratings of non-identifiers, Iain Gray received especially short shrift. His mean rating among these potentially 'floating voters' was, at 3.5, the lowest for any of the four Scottish leaders. We do not report a full breakdown by party identification because the story is a familiar one: partisans are naturally predisposed towards their own leader but some 'objectivity' shows through. SNP identifiers were by far the most positive about their own leader, rating Alex Salmond on average at 9.2.

That brings us to the main reason for the SNP's leadership advantage. We would normally expect incumbents to lose favour as they are at the mercy of political events and hence pay the 'costs of ruling' but a term as First Minister served to strengthen Salmond's popularity. This pushed him over the neutral point in the scale and thus well clear of all of the other ratings in the table. However, it is also worth recalling that the SNP's popularity boost outstripped Mr. Salmond's such that, like Mr. Gray, he was somewhat less popular than his party in 2011. One reason is that the First Minister continued to divide opinion: the standard deviation of Salmond's ratings is the highest in the table, indicating that he repelled many voters as well as attracting many others.

Tavish Scott looks to have suffered from the Liberal Democrats' general travails while Annabel Goldie remained a good deal better liked than her party – thus illustrating the limits on the capacity of a popular leader to salvage an unpopular party. Both leaders were viewed markedly more positively than their counterparts at Westminster. However, Iain Gray's unimpressive rating undermines any suggestion that there is a general bias in favour of Scottish leaders. Perhaps the most noticeable feature of the results for Mr Salmond's three challengers at Holyrood is the common non-response rate. Iain Gray's main problem looks to have been anonymity as much as unpopularity. Almost one in five respondents felt they knew too little about him to offer an opinion, and there were similar proportions for Tavish Scott and Annabel Goldie suggesting that the televised debates failed to provide a major platform for the party leaders. Judged by the frequency of 'don't know' responses, all five Westminster leaders proved at least as familiar as First Minister Salmond. The fact that Scottish voters have readier opinions on Westminster leaders indicates that these opinions were more influential on their vote choice though, at this stage, this is circumstantial evidence in that direction.

There is more suggestive evidence from another contrast between the results for Holyrood and Westminster leaders. For the three parties with both Scottish and British leaders, the correlation between leader and party effect is always stronger for the Westminster leader. That difference is large and statistically significant in the case of the Conservatives and Liberal Democrats and smaller for Labour (probably due to Ed Miliband's relative novelty at the time of the survey). In other words, it seems that parties are more readily associated in voters' minds with their UK leaders than with their Scottish leaders, even when these ratings are given in the run-up to a Holyrood election. This may in turn imply that the British party leaders were uppermost in voters' minds as they assessed the options in that election. If that is the case, then it was predictably bad news for the Westminster coalition parties but may have helped Labour, particularly if choices were influenced by sympathy for Gordon Brown and this is illustrated in his having the second highest mean rating of all nine leaders. Matters are different for the SNP, whose leader in Holyrood is unambiguously its pre-eminent figure. This may explain why the strongest correlation is between ratings of Alex Salmond and the SNP. Nonetheless, the sheer strength of that correlation ($r = 0.87$) warrants further explanation. It suggests that Salmond has become such a prominent and dominant figure within his party that the two are almost seen as interchangeable or equivalent in voters' minds.

A strong correlation cannot confirm the direction of causal relations between party and leader evaluations. Are voters' feelings about the SNP driven by their attitude towards its leader, or are their views of Salmond largely driven by their views of his party and, for example, its flagship constitutional policy? The answer is almost certainly 'both' but the predominant direction is of obvious importance because it determines the scope for leadership effects on voting behaviour. If leaders are judged by their parties, then evaluations of those leaders will not make an independent contribution to predicting attitudes to, and eventually choice between, those parties. So, one way of resolving the issue of causal direction is to see whether leader evaluations do make such an independent contribution to predicting party choice. If they do, then parties are being judged at least partly on the basis of their leaders.

Leadership evaluations and party choice

We test for this using the method of multinomial logistic regression that was introduced in Chapter 2. In that chapter, we presented a model including the core demographic and socio-economic variables that are at the beginning of the causal chain or 'funnel of causality' (Campbell et al. 1960) that drives voting behaviour. The regression analysis presented below includes all of those variables but here they serve as controls, allowing us to make cleaner estimates of the effect of leader evaluations. For example, it may be that working-class Scots have a distaste both for David Cameron and the Conservative Party. If we omit social class from our analysis, and consider only the leader evaluation and the vote, we risk concluding that the evaluation rather than social class is the causal force. We also include party identification as a control variable and for the same reason: it is a factor that is likely both to shape leader evaluations and to influence vote choice. A trickier question is whether to include the party like-dislike ratings. Including them creates a stiff test of whether leaders have a direct effect on voting choice, independent of their impact on the party's likeability, but it also conceals the potential indirect effect: we would not know whether the effect of party likeability was the result of other factors or of how that leader had shaped his or her party. The easiest way round this is to do both: to report models with and without the party evaluations. Explaining the differences between the results also helps to clarify the rather complicated logic behind the previous few sentences.

All nine leaders rated in Table 3.7 are included in the analysis. This enables us to assess the relative importance of Scottish and UK leaders on the choices made in 2011. The impact of a leader's evaluation on regional list vote is denoted by the size of the bars in Figure 3.2. While the full results of the regression are reported in Appendix 2 Table A2 3.1, the chart illustrates the effects of each leadership evaluation variable on predicted probabilities of the dependent variable. As in Chapter 2, the specific effect calculated is the change in predicted probability associated with a full range (0–10) change in that leader rating. In this multinomial context, there are multiple effect sizes for each predictor (reflecting the multiple coefficients: Lab vs. Con, Lab vs. Lib Dem, Lab vs. SNP) and so the changes in predicted probabilities are averaged across the three. Two effect sizes are calculated, reflecting the earlier discussion about whether party evaluations should be controlled when calculating leadership effects. The 'net' (or direct) effect is calculated from the models including those evaluations; the 'gross' (direct and indirect) effect is from models with party ratings omitted. To save lots of cross-checking with the model in Appendix A2 3.1, statistical significance is shown graphically: where none of the three coefficients for that leader was significant at the $p < 0.05$ level, the effect size bar has been made transparent.

The 'gross' effects in the chart are very large. This is partly because a full range change in these independent variables is a major change:

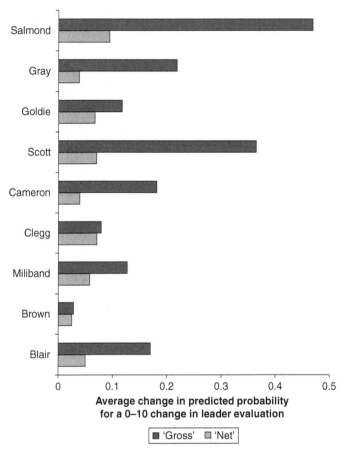

Figure 3.2 Mean effects of leadership evaluations on party choice
Sources: Pre- and post-election surveys.

we would expect those who strongly dislike a party's leader to be much less likely to support that party than those who strongly like it. Most respondents fall into the intermediate categories anyway, often at or near the midpoint. Even controlling for party identification, leader evaluations help us considerably in predicting voters' choices. They also reveal two important comparative conclusions. Perhaps reflecting his prominence in the campaign, it was attitudes to Alex Salmond that were the best predictors of choice in 2011 and, unlike in 2007, voting behaviour was overall better predicted by attitudes to the leaders at Holyrood than by attitudes to key figures at Westminster. In particular, and dashing the hopes for Labour raised earlier in the chapter, attitudes to Gordon Brown proved to have no significant relationship with party choice in 2011. Sympathy there may have been, but it did not translate into votes.

The 'net' effects of leadership, controlling for attitudes to the leaders' parties, are much weaker in almost all cases. This does not mean that leaders are unimportant. For one thing, most of the effects remain statistically significant and several are far from negligible in size. They are just dwarfed by the gross effects that now look suspiciously large, as if they were mainly a reflection of those partisan attitudes that are now controlled. The Salmond effect remains strong enough to suggest that the SNP benefited from the increase in his personal popularity compared to 2007. Secondly, a weaker 'net' effect leaves open the possibility of a strong but indirect impact of leadership. If Alex Salmond's major contribution was to boost the electability of the SNP, then the 'net' effect simply records that extra impact on voting of his polarizing image. As we have stressed, the causality could run the other way – that is, from party to leader evaluations. It seems likely, for example, that the apparently strong effect of attitudes to Tavish Scott was due to the fact that many voters simply projected their probably negative attitude to the Liberal Democrats onto the party's less familiar leader. There are two exceptions to the general rule that 'net' effects are far weaker. Controlling for partisan attitudes leaves in place much of the effect of attitudes to Annabel Goldie, indicating that she had carved out an image distinct from that of her party. Less easily explicable is the fact that ratings of Nick Clegg were barely affected by controlling for attitudes to the Liberal Democrats. It may be that he personally was blamed more than his party for the decision to join the Conservatives in coalition at Westminster. The Alternative Vote referendum held on the same day as the Scottish Parliament elections returned Clegg to the public spotlight, potentially reawakening awareness of the Liberal Democrats' leader. He remains an exception to the rule highlighted above. Whether we consider 'gross' or 'net' effects on voting, the Scottish leaders proved more influential than the British leaders in 2011. This introduces a theme that will recur in Chapter 5.

Conclusion

Labour entered the election year of 2011 with grounds for confidence. It had polled strongly in Scotland at the general election in 2010 and, following its replacement with a Conservative-led coalition at Westminster, had enjoyed a resurgence in Holyrood voting intentions. The party began to look likely to become the largest party at Holyrood following the 2011 elections. One of the bases for such optimism was made clear in this chapter. In terms of enduring partisan identities, Labour seems to be comfortably better off than any of its rivals. If regarded as a 'core vote', this bloc of self-proclaimed Labour supporters provided at least the basis for the victory charge in 2011. We return to this issue in Chapter 5.

The evidence presented in this chapter highlights three key reasons why that victory did not materialize. First, Labour's base did not serve as a 'core vote': many Labour identifiers abstained or even voted for other parties. Secondly, party identification is not just a matter of enduring attachments that voters learn early and stick to from then on. There are other considerations that influence vote choices, including the perceived performance, policies and leadership. Moreover, since these short-term factors differ across electoral context (for example, a party might have a more popular leader at Westminster than at Holyrood), we cannot expect attachments formed in one context to be important in another. Thirdly, party identifiers form only around half of the electorate and so even a dominant position among that group takes a party only so far towards the electoral winning-line. Election outcomes are ultimately determined by the competing parties' appeal to the unattached voters.

In 2007, Labour's stronger support base was almost but not quite enough to outweigh the SNP's advantage in more immediate popularity. By 2011, that SNP advantage had widened considerably and so in turn did the party's margin of victory. Both the party and its leader had become more popular. This is notable not least because it bucks the 'cost of ruling' (Nannestad and Paldam 2000) trend that sees a general downward drift in the popularity of governing parties and leaders. Incumbents often recover from mid-term blues but rarely to the point of surpassing their showing at the previous election, let alone achieving the double-digit gains that the SNP managed in 2011. So how did the SNP turn the potential disadvantage of governing, during a difficult economic and fiscal period and without an overall majority, into an advantage? One part of the answer lies in the SNP's performance in office. As we see in the next chapter, voters were on the whole impressed by the government's record. Yet the basis for such evaluations is not always obvious. Voters keep no more than half on eye on the detail of government activity (see Delli Carpini and Keeter 1996). This is where party image comes in. Voters' performance evaluations are driven as much by their general impression of a party as by specifics of its policies and record (Crewe 1988: 49), and the results in this chapter show that the SNP gave by far the most favourable impression to voters in 2011. Two aspects of that image – capacity for strong government and standing up for Scotland – are particularly important and we examine both in the next chapter. The SNP's appeal was more general and it even trumped Labour on a characteristic, being in touch with ordinary people, that might be thought of as central to the latter's traditional 'brand'. Party image has been largely neglected in studies of British electoral behaviour – surprisingly so, given that politics is often characterised as image-dominated. Yet such studies as there are, whether recent (Andersen and Evans 2003) or not so recent (Butler and Stokes 1974; Bennie et al. 1997), indicate that such images have a marked influence on voters' behaviour. In our full models of party choice in Chapter 6, we examine whether the same was true in Scotland in 2011. If so, it will have worked strongly in the SNP's favour.

4

Performance Politics at Holyrood

'What policies politicians follow is their business; what they accomplish is the voter's business' (Fiorina 1981: 13). This sums up the 'performance politics' model of voting that, in a series of publications, Harold Clarke and his British Election Study colleagues argue is the key to understanding recent British general elections (Clarke et al. 2004, 2009, 2011). In this approach, also known as the valence model, there is broad agreement among parties, if not voters, about the desired outcomes of policy. Electoral competition is thus about which contender for office is most likely to deliver. The notion of 'performance politics' is rooted in models of retrospective voting developed for US elections by Downs (1957), Key (1966) and Fiorina (1981) in which presidents and executives are rewarded or punished according to their record in office. Voters assess whether the incumbent has performed satisfactorily and, if not, whether it seems likely that the challenger would have done any better.

In line with Fiorina's dictum, few voters have anything more than minimal awareness of the specific policies outlined in the parties' manifestos at a given election and few have strong opinions about those policies (Converse 1964; Zaller 1992). But it is misleading to suggest that there is public agreement on objectives and disagreement only on the party thought best able to achieve them. There are broad ideological differences within the British, and Scottish, electorate, most notably in terms of the left-right dimension that has been the main basis of party competition for the past century. Voters may skate over the policy detail but most will have at least some general view on, for example, how far government should intervene in the economy. However, these differences in core values or principles can only determine voting behaviour insofar as the parties themselves differ on the same lines. So one key reason why the 'performance politics' model has currency in Britain is that, especially since 'New' Labour's shift to the centre ground, policy differences between the major parties have narrowed (Green 2007; Paterson 2006). If the major contenders are agreed on what should be done, voters are left only to judge which party is best equipped to do it. A second reason why the valence model has gained explanatory power is partisan de-alignment. As we saw in Chapter 3, while many voters feel at least some lingering connection to a particular party, these ties have loosened considerably over the past few decades and may not deserve to be called 'loyalties' given the willingness of identifiers to abstain or even to defect to other parties at election time. Less partisan voters are more likely to make a late decision about how to vote and more likely to be swayed by short-term factors such as government performance.

It is useful here to introduce a distinction between explaining *individual votes* and explaining *election outcomes*. Long-term partisan or ideological identifications can explain the choices of many individuals within the electorate but such factors are generally static: they account for people voting the same way at election after election. In the Scottish context, an important example is constitutional preference. This influences voting behaviour – staunch opponents of independence are unlikely to vote SNP while many staunch supporters of independence would never vote any other way. Such strongly held opinions are very unlikely to change between elections. By contrast, perceptions of government performance – and related components of the 'performance politics' model such as leader evaluations and party image – fluctuate much more and tend, therefore, to be what swings the election outcome. The central argument of this book is that this is what happened in 2011. In concluding the previous chapter, we suggested a 'performance politics' explanation of the marked increase in like-dislike ratings for both the SNP and its First Minister. We have already seen that most voters were convinced of the party's capacity for strong government, and many trusted the SNP to keep its promises. In this chapter, we look in more detail at voters' assessment of the government's record. Particular attention is paid to the economy, which, understandably given the context, elbowed most other issues off the agenda. The economic difficulties, and particularly the consequences for Scotland of the UK government's fiscal retrenchment, provide a useful illustration of the specific way in which the valence model operates in Scottish elections. Part of what it means 'to perform well' for a Scottish government is to manage relations with Westminster in a way that defends Scottish interests. The SNP's strong reputation in this regard was a cornerstone of its electoral success in 2011.

Assessing the government's record

The valence model envisages voters assessing past and future performance in office. As such, it also implies that voters are primarily focused on those parties with a realistic chance of governing. Identifying likely parties of government is generally more difficult in a multi-party system under proportional representation, as exists in devolved elections in Scotland, than in a simpler party system under majoritarian rules, as in elections to the House of Commons. Despite the current role-reversal (with a coalition at Westminster and majority government at Holyrood), a more proportional system is more likely to result in a coalition as occurred following the first two Scottish elections. However, predicting both the likely coalition permutations and their potential performance is well beyond the commitment and knowledge of most voters. Whether anticipating future performance or administering credit or blame for past performance, voters usually focus on the larger parties that are the dominant coalition partners. The media do likewise. In 2011 (as in 2007), the election was presented as a battle for government between Labour and the SNP despite the fact that, at least until very late in the campaign, neither party was thought to have a realistic prospect of winning an overall majority. This tendency to focus on the two largest parties may have been reinforced by the formation of an SNP minority government in 2007. Neither the SNP nor Labour were under pressure to explain whether or with whom they would coalesce during the election campaign despite reports suggesting that both the Liberal Democrats and Greens were willing to reach agreement with Labour. Given the focus on them as the two potential (main) governing parties, in this section our main concern is with the SNP and Labour.

One contrast between 2007 and 2011 is that, by the time of the latter election, most Scots had experience of both leading parties in office. This makes it easier to assess their valence credentials. If a party has been out of power for a decade or more then estimating performance is difficult, leaving voters to rely heavily on less direct evidence such as party image and leader evaluations (Butt 2006). However, in 2011 there was a relatively recent history of Labour in power (though as the larger party in coalition), which will have helped Scots to judge how the party would have performed had it won the 2007 election. It might be wondered why we are focusing on past performance, whether real or estimated, given that voting is about choosing a future government. As Clarke et al. (2004: 26) put it, '[r]ational voters have no interest in rewarding or punishing anybody'. Yet the past is often voters' most reliable guide to the future – especially given public scepticism about the value of parties' promises. As Downs put it, the voter:

> must either compare (1) two hypothetical future utility incomes or (2) one actual present utility income and one hypothetical present one. Without question, the latter comparison allows him, to make more direct use of concrete facts than the former. Not only is one of its terms a real entity, but the other can be calculated in full view of the situation from which it springs.
>
> (1957: 40)

Knowing the context in which a Labour-led Scottish government would have been operating, voters can assess how its performance would compare with that of the SNP administration. Hence our core measures of perceived performance are retrospective: 'How good or bad a job of running Scotland do you think SNP ministers in the Scottish Government have done since 2007?' and 'If Labour had been leading the Scottish Government over the past four years, how good or bad a job of running Scotland do you think they would have done?'

Table 4.1 shows voters' assessments alongside, for the purposes of comparison, performance evaluations for the outgoing and incoming Westminster governing parties. It is clear that voters were relatively impressed by the performance of the SNP minority government. Indeed, since even popular governments usually win grudging

Table 4.1 Evaluations of governing party performance: Scottish and Westminster governments

	How good a job done by...				
	Scottish government		Westminster government		
	SNP 2007–2011 %	Labour if in power %	Labour 1997–2010 %	Con 2010– %	Lib Dem 2010– %
Very good	14	4	5	4	1
Fairly good	42	27	31	18	13
Neither	25	26	19	23	23
Fairly bad	12	25	21	25	26
Very bad	8	18	25	30	36
Good – Bad	+36	−12	−10	−33	−48
N	1923	1613	1967	1951	1943

Note: The base N for the Labour at Holyrood assessment is lower because that question was taken from the post-election wave of the survey.
Source: Pre- and post-election surveys.

respect rather than lavish praise, the SNP's +36 rating (obtained by subtracting the two 'bad' percentages from the two 'good' percentages) is impressive. Notably, voters did not believe that Labour would have done an especially good job if in power at Holyrood. Indeed, the similarity of the Labour ratings for Westminster and Holyrood tends to belie any notion that Labour in Westminster was a drag on the party at Holyrood, or vice versa. Another similarity is with Labour's net rating of -14 from the equivalent retrospective evaluation question in the 2007 SES. While there are clearly other factors at play, the closeness of the 2003–2007 (actual) and 2007–2011 (hypothetical) ratings does suggest that voters drew on their recollections of Labour in office when forming their expectations of how Labour would have performed had it won in 2007.

In the light of the SNP-Labour gap in Table 4.1, a substantial victory for the former in 2011 is not hard to explain. While we do not have an exact comparison with an SNP overall performance evaluation from 2007, there is strong indirect evidence of change between the two elections that can explain the SNP's surge. Respondents in the 2007 SES were asked to rate Labour (actual) and SNP (hypothetical) performance in six issue areas (see Johns et al. 2009: 217–218). While the SNP led Labour on four of the six issues, these advantages were typically quite narrow, and are dwarfed by the difference in Table 4.1. In 2011, the SNP had pulled away from Labour to enjoy a clear and crucial competence advantage.

These evaluations are subjective and, in particular, they will be strongly influenced by partisan predispositions. Rather than presenting a full breakdown of the results by party identification, we pick out some specific statistics from that analysis. First, among non-identifiers, the SNP net rating was +38 while Labour's was −26. The fact that Labour's rating is more negative than that shown in Table 4.1 is not that surprising: non-identifiers have in a sense rejected the political parties and so we would expect them generally to take a more jaundiced view of likely performance. The striking result is that non-identifiers took just as positive a view of the SNP's record as the electorate as a whole. Second, apart from the Conservatives, all of the other groups of identifiers gave the SNP overall positive evaluations. Among self-proclaimed Labour supporters – that is, supporters of the SNP's main opposition party – the SNP received a net rating of +13. We have seen in previous chapters that the SNP was able to win votes across the socio-demographic and partisan board. The consistently favourable evaluations of the party's performance in government look a likely reason for this.

What, then, were the drivers of these positive evaluations? One way of addressing this question is to consider voters' assessments of outcomes in key policy areas. Voters were asked whether the standard of health in Scotland had increased or fallen since 2007. The same question was then asked about education, standards of living, and law and order. Responses are reported in Table 4.2, along with the kind of net rating (per cent 'increased' minus per cent 'fallen') calculated in the previous table.

Most respondents were willing to offer an assessment on most of the issue areas. Only in the field of education, with which many people have little or no direct contact, did fewer than seven in eight respondents express no opinion. Those who did offer a view were seldom very complimentary. The most clearly negative figure can be heavily discounted because, as we see shortly, the Scottish government was largely exempted from blame for a plunge in living standards experienced far beyond Scotland. But, in the three major devolved issue domains of health, education, and law and order,

Table 4.2   Evaluations of outcomes in four key issue areas

	Health (% DK = 9) %	Education (% DK = 23) %	Living standards (% DK = 7) %	Law and order (% DK = 12) %
Increased a lot	5	3	1	4
Increased a little	27	19	13	20
Stayed the same	41	38	27	40
Fallen a little	18	28	40	23
Fallen a lot	8	11	19	13
Increased – Fallen	+6	−17	−44	−11
N	1832	1571	1897	1763

Source: Pre-election survey.

assessments were at best mixed and, on balance, negative. Pluralities in all three cases detected no change. In short, Table 4.2 is of little help in accounting for the strongly positive assessments of the SNP's record in office.

There are a number of potential explanations for the discrepancy between the issue outcomes and the overall evaluation. It might be that voters' expectations of government performance are so low that 'no change' is regarded as something of a triumph. Another point, discussed in the previous chapter, is that voters incorporate little detail on policy and outcomes into their overall assessments of a party, relying instead on broad impressions of party image and heuristics such as leadership evaluations. Thirdly, it may be that the issues in Table 4.2 were not those uppermost in voters' minds when assessing the SNP, and voting, in 2011. We address that issue in the next section on issue salience. Meanwhile, we consider a final possibility: that, as with living standards, the Scottish government tended to escape the blame for negative evaluations.

That hypothesis is tested using a follow-up to the questions set out in Table 4.2. Having reported their assessment of outcomes, respondents were asked for each issue: 'And is this mainly the result of: (i) the policies of the UK government at Westminster; (ii) the policies of the Scottish Government; (iii) both equally; (iv) some other reason?' We look at these questions in detail in Chapter 5, assessing the extent to which the different governments were being

Table 4.3 Attributions of responsibility for outcomes in four issue areas by evaluations

	Health			Education		
	UK	Scottish	N	UK	Scottish	N
Increased	4	96	489	4	96	309
Stayed the same	28	72	321	16	84	260
Fallen	52	48	233	31	69	404

	Living standards			Law and order		
	UK	Scottish	N	UK	Scottish	N
Increased	10	90	201	6	94	351
Stayed the same	33	67	193	20	80	254
Fallen	83	17	664	34	66	368

Source: Pre-election survey.

held to account in this Scottish Parliament election. Here, for the sake of simplicity and maximizing cell sizes, we confine analysis to those choosing one of the first two categories. For the same reasons, we also simplify the outcome evaluations into three-category variables. Table 4.3 shows the attributions of responsibility for each issue according to whether respondents had previously reported an improvement, a deterioration or no change.

In all four issue areas, those perceiving improvements overwhelmingly attributed these to the Scottish government. The less impressed the respondents, the more likely they were to blame the UK government. The extent to which blame was transferred may depend on how unambiguously devolved an issue is believed to be. On education and crime, even those perceiving deterioration thought that this fell within the Scottish government's remit. But declining living standards were in most cases blamed on the UK government, and presumably therefore on its economic management. The qualification reflects the ambiguity of 'living standards': they need not be confined to economic matters (and indeed might be influenced by developments in the other three issue areas). And it is noticeable that, in a time of economic gloom, substantial minorities reported their living standards to have improved or at least held steady. Still more striking is that those successes were mostly attributed to the

Scottish government. This is consistent with findings from the 2007 SES that, while voters tend to see Westminster as on balance more powerful in the economic domain, they also perceive the Holyrood government as fairly influential over economic outcomes (Johns et al. 2010: 139).

Our now oft-repeated acknowledgement of partisan bias is required here. SNP supporters are inclined to credit their government for successes and to exempt it from blame for failures. But there simply are not enough SNP supporters to generate the large and consistent differences in Table 4.3 and, of course, the Scottish government's opponents have the opposite partisan motivation. These results can only be explained if Scottish voters as a whole were prone to attribute improvements to the government at Holyrood and to blame problems on Westminster. This might be thought to be a general bias in favour of Scottish over UK institutions, perhaps driven by national rather than partisan identity. But it seems likely to be due at least in part to the gulf in overall competence evaluations between the SNP and the Westminster governing parties between 2007 and 2011 (see Table 4.1). Respondents with those general opinions of the Scottish and UK governments might reasonably have inferred that problems were the fault of the latter. As usual, the causal relations between general impressions and specific evaluations are hard to disentangle. What is clear is that Table 4.3 goes a long way to explain how the SNP was able to maintain a strong reputation for competence though not credited with major policy achievements.

Issue salience

As mentioned earlier, another possible reason why the SNP was able to overcome lacklustre ratings on health, education and crime is that these matters may not have been of much concern to voters in 2011. On the one hand this seems unlikely as these are bread-and-butter public service issues, routinely important in British elections anyway, and they are the most significant areas in which powers have been devolved to the Scottish Parliament. On the other hand, the economy had long dominated the political and media agenda in Scotland as in the rest of Britain. Scottish voters were no less affected by the crisis for the fact that the macro-economic levers were still pulled in London or elsewhere. With constitutional arrangements and context pulling in opposite directions, the 2011 election makes for an interesting case study of issue salience.

Issue importance was addressed in two ways in the 2011 SES. In the pre-election survey, we asked respondents about the most important problems facing first Scotland and then the UK. Analysis of those results follows in the next chapter, in the multi-level context of the election. Here, we focus on a question from the post-election survey that asks more directly about electoral salience. Respondents offered a broad range of answers in explaining what they regarded as the single most important issue in deciding how they had voted in response to an open-ended question: 'What was the *single most important issue* for you when deciding how to vote in the Scottish Parliament election?' [emphasis in the original question]. This was an open-ended question and, as we shall see, respondents took advantage of the full rein this gave them to say whatever was on their mind. Digesting this rich variety of responses requires us to code them into categories. Table 4.4 compares the answers given in 2011 with those given in 2007 using the same coding scheme developed for the previous election. In the

Table 4.4 Open-ended 'most important issue' responses, 2007 and 2011

	2007 %	2011 %	Change 2007–2011
Constitutional question	26	15	−11
Council tax	9	3	−6
Health	7	2	−5
Crime	7	2	−5
Education	6	4	−2
Economy	6	33	+27
Defence/military	5	1	−4
Environment/energy	3	0	−3
Others	31	39	+8
Other specific issues		7	
Parties – general		13	
Government record		5	
Scottish interests		10	
Leaders		3	
Local candidate		2	
N	916	1134	

Source: Post-election surveys, 2007 and 2011.

upper rows we present a comparison based on the issues mentioned most often across the two elections. Non-responses such as 'don't know' or 'none' are omitted from the analysis.[1] The pattern is clear. Not only was the economy far more salient in 2011 than it had been in 2007 but it gained importance at the expense of all other issues. Some of these, like the environment and Britain's military action in Iraq and Afghanistan, slipped almost completely off the electorate's agenda. The constitutional question remained important relative to other issues – as in 2007, it was mentioned more often than health, education and crime combined but now fewer than one in six voters described it as the key driver of their choice, compared to one in three citing the broad category of the economy. Whether we are able to conclude from this question that independence was less important to voters in 2011 than in 2007 depends on whether we are referring to relative or absolute importance: that is, whether salience is regarded as a zero-sum game whereby, given a limited amount of public attention, greatly heightened concern with one issue inevitably means that others fall down the agenda or if the public's attention can expand, allowing some issues to gain in importance while others retain their position. While that difficult question is well beyond this book (but see Wlezien, 2005), we can at least say that a party seen as strong on the economy but more vulnerable on the constitutional question would, other things remaining the same, fare better in the 2011 than in the 2007 election.

Aside from the economy, the only other category that grew in importance in 2011 was the clustering of 'Other' responses. It is worth examining this category in more detail, partly because of its size – accounting for almost 40 per cent of all responses – but also because it is less heterogeneous than might be thought. What is striking about these 'Other' responses is that only a relatively small proportion (less than 20 per cent of the 'Other' category and hence only 7 per cent of responses overall) referred to specific issues in the way envisaged by those designing the 'most important issue' question (see Wlezien 2005). Many gave responses with no content other than the mention of parties or leaders and many more gave what might be called 'general valence' responses, either commenting on the government's record or on their chosen party's capacity to promote or protect Scottish interests. Many of these 'Other' responses thus provide unusually direct evidence of valence voting. They also highlight a specifically Scottish dimension to 'performance politics'. The reason why issue salience matters is that the outcome of an electoral contest depends in large part on the territory over which it is fought. Having reported their 'most important issue', respondents were then asked to name the party, if any, they deemed 'best able to handle that issue'. The multiplicity of issues mentioned means that cell sizes quickly become quite small and so, in Table 4.5, we focus only on those 'issues' – broadly defined and thus including the vaguer and more valence-type considerations mentioned just above – that were cited by at least 40 respondents.

Two thirds (66 per cent) of those nominating the constitution as most important issue declared the SNP was the best party to handle it. The corresponding figure in the 2007 SES was 50 per cent. In other words, among those voting on the constitution, the proportion of independence supporters has increased, and the proportion voting to try to stop independence has decreased. It is the latter more than the former that seems to have been distracted by the economy. That differential will obviously have worked in the SNP's favour, as will the party's relatively strong showing on the economy. There may have been doubt about how much any Scottish government could

Table 4.5 Party best able to handle each 'most important issue', row percentages

	None	Con	Lab	LD	SNP	Other	DK	N
Constitution	2	12	14	1	66	2	3	173
Education	5	5	29	2	56	0	2	41
Economy	5	11	25	2	45	1	11	286
Unemployment	0	2	46	2	42	0	8	48
Public finances	5	24	29	2	27	2	10	41
Parties – general	8	9	19	3	55	1	5	154
Government record	2	0	7	0	88	2	2	56
Scottish interests	2	0	2	0	95	0	1	107
All issues	5	9	20	2	55	3	6	1132

Source: Post-election survey.

do to influence macro-economic outcomes but, of the alternatives for office, the SNP was clearly the plurality preference. This is consistent with the earlier results on attributions of responsibility (Table 4.3), which showed that the Scottish government tended to receive credit but avoid blame for changes in living standards. The SNP-Labour battle was a lot closer on more specific economic matters like unemployment and the public finances.[2] However, given that these are traditional Labour strengths and, in the case of protecting the public sector, also major campaign themes in 2011, the lack of any significant advantage over the SNP is notable. Education, another of Labour's chosen battlegrounds, was an issue on which the SNP enjoyed a large lead. In short, it is hard to identify an SNP weak point in Table 4.5. The party may have been vulnerable on other issues, like law and order, but these were not high enough on voters' agenda to cause serious problems in 2011.

But the most obvious advantage for the SNP lies not with specific issues but on the more general valence criteria in the lower rows of the table. The 'best party to handle' follow-up question becomes almost superfluous when the reported 'most important issue' is simply the approval of a party, its record or its commitment to Scottish interests. The key point here is that, in the large majority of cases, that party was the SNP. Virtually no one commented adversely on the SNP government's record. There were many more 'keep Labour out' than 'get the SNP out' responses and the SNP had a monopoly in the 'Scottish interests' category. All of this reinforces our argument that positive evaluations of the SNP were based more on general impressions of competence and commitment to Scottish interests than on their record or policies on specific issues. A final point to note is that, especially in a post-election survey, the 'party best to handle' responses are inevitably prone to rationalization. It might seem perverse to choose a different party from the one voted for just a day or so before. Yet the proportions in the final 'All issues' row do not simply replicate the vote shares. Clearly, some people voted for other parties, perhaps out of loyalty, fear of independence or for some other reason despite having nominated the SNP as best able to handle their agenda-topping issue. This echoes the persistent finding from Chapter 3: the election outcome reflected the partial cancelling of the SNP's disadvantage in terms of longstanding predispositions and its major advantage in terms of short-term popularity and competence.

Issues, policies and performance

So far, in discussing valence politics, we have used the term to refer to voters choosing the party they see as generally most competent. Yet the term 'valence' originated as a description for particular issues (Stokes 1963, 1992): that is, those on which voters and parties share the same objectives, and so issue competition revolves around which party is likeliest to achieve them. The quintessential example is economic prosperity: everyone wants it but the question is which party will deliver it. Valence issues are to be distinguished from position issues, on which voters, and potentially parties, take different positions and have different policy preferences. A prominent position issue at the 2007 Scottish Parliament election (see Table 4.4) was that of whether the council tax should be retained (as argued by Labour and the Conservatives) or replaced by a local income tax (favoured by the SNP and the Liberal Democrats).

The distinction is useful but is overdrawn if used to classify entire policy areas as valence or position (Stokes 1963: 373). Any issue has both valence and positional components, because even with shared objectives there is considerable potential to disagree about the policies necessary to achieve them. The recession overshadowing recent elections provides a good example. Some argue that the route to growth is fiscal retrenchment in order to assuage market fears, keep interest rates low and tackle debt. Others favour a more expansionary fiscal policy in order to boost employment and increase the ratio of tax revenue to benefit expenditure. As Table 4.6 shows, the Scottish electorate was divided on that question and on several other policy issues that were at stake in the 2011 election.[3] The electorate might be unified in its wish for lower crime, improved health provision and so on, but they do not agree about the best means of achieving those ends. Even if the balance of opinion was usually clear – though this was least so on that fiscal policy question – there was always a substantial minority dissenting from the general view.

Why, then, did most of these issues rarely if ever appear in 'most important issue' responses? And why has it become customary in British electoral studies to characterize domains like law and order, education and health as valence issues (e.g. Clarke et al. 2004, 2009)? One reason is summarized by Fiorina quoted in the opening sentence of this chapter. In essence, voters eschew policy detail and focus on

Table 4.6   Distribution of voters' opinions on six policy issues

	Agree	Neither	Disagree	N
For less serious offences, shorter, community sentences should replace imprisonment	55	15	30	1973
Free medical prescriptions for all should be abolished	31	11	57	1996
The Scottish government should make more use of tax varying powers to raise revenue	50	23	27	1871
Mandatory prison sentences for anyone found carrying a knife should be used to cut down on knife crime	67	13	20	1984
University students should contribute to the costs of their education after graduation	56	15	29	1986
In the current economic climate, the government should maintain the size of the public sector	46	20	34	1901

Source: Pre-election survey.

broad outcomes. But, as the example of local taxation in 2007 makes clear, a divisive issue made prominent by a party and media will register with significant numbers of voters. The other key reason for the dominance of valence competition in the 2011 election is the lack of positional differences between the parties. However strongly a voter feels on a policy issue, it cannot determine their vote if they are choosing between parties with the same position on that issue (see Butler and Stokes 1974: 276–295). Returning to the example of fiscal policy, it is instructive to compare 2011 with the UK general election the previous year. The two leading contenders in the general election, the Conservatives and Labour, took a different view on the final statement in Table 4.6, giving this highly salient issue the potential to shape voting behaviour. In the 2011 election, however, Labour and the SNP and, for that matter, the Liberal Democrats were hard to separate on fiscal policy. Only the Conservatives deviated from the consensus against cuts. As a result, only the choices of those willing to contemplate a Conservative vote, a small proportion of the Scottish electorate, could be influenced by the debt reduction issue. The rest had to find another basis for choosing between the remaining options.

This is borne out by evidence from the 2011 SES. Respondents were asked to locate the parties on two 0–10 issue placement scales: from 'cut taxes a lot and spend much less on public services' to 'raise taxes a lot and spend much more on public services'; and from 'abolishing the Scottish Parliament and returning to pre-devolution arrangements' to 'independence for Scotland'. Figure 4.1 shows the distribution of voters' self-placements and also their mean placements of the four main parties for each statement. The two graphs are in sharp contrast. In the tax-spending case, three of the four main parties, including the main two contenders, were clustered closely together. Only the Conservatives were seen as offering anything remotely distinctive on that dimension. Because many voters were also located at or near the middle point of the scale, it makes sense from the parties' point of view to position themselves in the same area. While the tax-spending issue was very prominent in the 2011 campaign, albeit often in the context of Westminster's budget decisions, there was little scope for policy voting in that domain. Self-placements on the constitutional issue range more widely than those on taxes and spending, with large minorities in both extreme positions, but the more striking polarization is among the political parties, which between them cover almost the entire scale rather than huddling in the middle. This means that there is more scope for constitutional preferences to drive voting behaviour, and Table 4.4 suggests that this happened.

The proximity of Labour and the SNP in Figure 4.1(i) is an illustration of the ideological convergence that has characterized Scottish politics over many years, especially now that Labour and the SNP are clearly the dominant forces. The two have traditionally had similar policies and adjacent stances on the left-right spectrum and the SNP eventually followed Labour in its move to the right in the 1990s. Thus, at each of the Scottish Parliament elections so far, voters' left-right position proved not to be a significant predictor of choice between the two parties (Paterson et al. 2001: chs. 4, 8; Paterson 2006; Johns et al. 2010, ch. 10). The only appreciable ideological difference remains the gap between these parties and the Conservatives who, as indicated in Figure 4.1(i), are perceived to have maintained a centre-right position (Bennie et al. 1997; Paterson 2006).

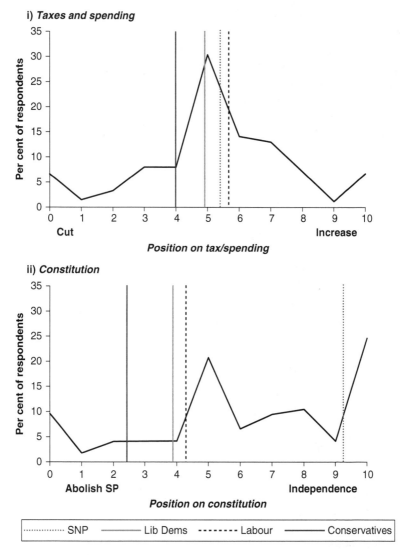

Figure 4.1 Voter self-placements and mean party placements on two issue scales

Source: Pre-election survey.

In addition to the issue placement scales, 2011 SES respondents were asked, 'Considering everything that the SNP and the Labour party stand for, how much difference would you say there is between them?' Most voters acknowledged at least some difference between the two main parties: 52 per cent choosing either 'a great deal' or 'quite a lot'. What we have seen suggests that these responses are driven largely by positions on the central question of the constitution. Some indirect evidence supporting that suggestion comes from a comparison with the 2007 survey in which the equivalent percentage was 68 per cent. This is not because the parties have converged on the constitutional question but instead reflects the salience shifts observed in Table 4.4. The most important issues in 2011 were economic matters on which Labour and the SNP did not advocate significantly different policies or approaches, though there were perceived differences in levels of competence. The constitutional issue, however, which really divides the parties, was less prominent in voters' thinking.

This is not to say that matters of tax and spending were irrelevant in the 2011 election. However, in the absence of broad policy differences between the main parties, the valence aspects of an issue – that is, which party will handle it best – come to the fore. What it means to 'handle' an issue depends on the context and, in particular, on the extent to which the Scottish government is perceived as making policy itself or as reacting to policies made by the UK government. Given the financial regime governing the Scottish government, major decisions on revenues and expenditures are taken at Westminster. In valence terms, the Scottish parties in 2011 would be judged first on their capacity to minimize the constraints placed on the Scottish government, and second on their ability to manage within those constraints. Our characterization of this as a valence issue is consistent with its treatment by the parties, especially the SNP and Labour, during the campaign. They competed explicitly on the question of who would best defend Scotland against the expenditure-cutting agenda of the UK's coalition government.

The upper panel of Table 4.7 shows results to a question asking about the effectiveness of the different parties in managing the impact of cuts from Westminster. Labour was given some credit for its ability to defend Scotland against the impact of the UK government's cuts: 48 per cent of respondents expected the party to be 'very' or

Table 4.7 Perception of parties' commitment to defending (i) Scotland against the cuts; (ii) Scottish interests in general

		Con %	Lab %	Lib Dem %	SNP %
i) Managing impact of cuts					
Very effective		7	10	2	18
Fairly effective		24	38	20	46
Not very effective		31	30	40	22
Not at all effective		38	21	38	14
N		1,701	1,704	1,678	1,702
ii) Look after Scottish interests					
Very closely		3	9	2	58
Fairly closely		15	45	30	32
Not very closely		36	31	43	6
Not at all closely		47	15	24	3
2011	Mean	1.7	2.5	2.1	3.5
	N	1,529	1,536	1,492	1,574
2007	Mean	2.0	2.4	2.5	3.0
	N	1,353	1,377	1,333	1,353
iii) Correlation between i) and ii)					
Kendall's tau-c		0.47	0.44	0.37	0.37
N		1383	1390	1352	1408

Sources: 2011 pre- and post-election surveys; 2007 post-election survey.

'fairly' effective in this respect. However, in fighting the campaign on that issue, the party was triumphing only over the Westminster coalition parties, who were already defeated on this issue. This was fertile territory for the SNP, which, judging by these data, had successfully positioned itself as Scotland's strongest defence against what were widely seen as 'London's cuts'. If managing the impact of budget cuts was a particularly important test of competence in 2011, the SNP passed that test comfortably ahead of its rivals.

A similar story can be told about the second part of the table. It reports responses to a more general question about how closely the parties look after Scottish interests. In addition to the distribution of responses, mean scores are provided, based on coding the scale from 1 ('not at all closely') to 4 ('very closely'), to enable an economical comparison with 2007 ratings. Again, Labour outperforms the coalition parties on this criterion, but not by the margin it might have hoped for and with little sign of improvement from 2007: Labour's mean score lifted only from 2.4 to 2.5 (the middle point of the scale). This undermines any ideas that the key to Labour's rating is whether they are in power at Westminster. It suggests that Labour needs more than the election of a Conservative-led government in London in order to regain its reputation for defending Scotland. Unsurprisingly, given the results on the 'standing up for Scotland' party image question (see Table 3.4), by far the strongest 'Scottish interest' ratings were for the SNP. Not only that but it was the SNP that gained significant ground between 2007 and 2011. It is hard to say whether the SNP's improved reputation is due to events at Westminster, to their record in office at Holyrood or both. In any case, to the extent that the 2011 election was about who would defend Scottish interests, it was the SNP that stood to gain.

In the final rows of the table, we report the correlation between the two ratings for each party: on defending Scotland against the cuts and on general concern for Scottish interests. Not surprisingly, all of the correlations are positive and fairly strong. They key point for present purposes, however, is that they are not very strong. Some voters may infer the specific issue stance from the general commitment (and others do the reverse), these are distinct evaluations and thus each had the potential to influence voting behaviour in 2011. Analysis of the 2007 survey shows that the general Scottish interests ratings were a powerful influence over party choice in that election (Johns et al. 2010, ch. 10), and there is no reason to suppose that things have changed in 2011. Yet, even taking these ratings into account, our prediction of party choice may be further improved by knowing how voters rate the parties on the specific matter of 'defending Scotland against the cuts'. We test that hypothesis via the full vote models in the final chapter.

The constitutional issue in 2011

No one should doubt the enduring prominence of the constitutional question in Scottish politics. In particular, it might be assumed that both support for and opposition to the SNP is driven largely by constitutional preferences. Supporters of independence continue to comprise the SNP's core vote, and the 'most important issue' responses confirm that part of the electorate votes against the SNP with the aim of preventing independence. However, there are two important points to note about those who vote primarily on the constitutional issue. First, they are clearly in the minority. Secondly, their votes are quite predictable, such that their behaviour cannot explain the kind of swings in vote shares seen in Scottish Parliament elections since 1999. In particular, there are compelling reasons to believe that the constitutional issue contributed only minimally to explaining the surge in SNP support between 2007 and 2011 that gave the party its majority.

One reason was shown in Table 4.4: the constitution was a less salient issue in 2011 than at the previous election. As the economy grew in importance at this election, it is the more likely source of the SNP's electoral advance. The declining salience of the constitutional issue might be seen as a consequence not only of the economic context but also of the SNP's campaigning, which, since devolution, has not centred on independence but emphasizes the party's governing competence. The success of this strategy is indicated by responses to SES question: 'How do you think that the return of an SNP minority government would affect the likelihood of independence?' Only 7 per cent of respondents thought that independence was 'much more likely' with the return of an SNP minority government and the largest group (42 per cent) thought that it would 'make no difference'. What might have once been a major deterrent to voting SNP, the fear of independence, is now less of a source of anxiety and concern within the electorate. By easing concerns about the constitutional issue, the SNP were able to take fuller advantage of the other factors, such as competence, leadership and image, which are the more likely sources of its advance in 2011.

But the clearest evidence that the constitution did not drive the 2011 outcome comes from the stability of constitutional preferences themselves. Table 4.8 presents two measures of constitutional preferences. The first is a simplified version of a long-running Scottish survey question, which offers respondents five options ranging from abolition of the Scottish Parliament to independence outside the European Union.[4] This question has the particular advantage of longevity, enabling comparison across time. However, it is supplemented by a newer question that more closely reflects current debate on the issue. This question is in the form of a hypothetical referendum vote with three options: the status quo ('Keep the Scottish

Table 4.8 Two measures of constitutional preference at Scottish elections since 1999

	1999 %	2003 %	2007 %	2011 %
Five-option question				
Independence (in or out of EU)	28	28	25	26
Devolution (with or without tax powers)	62	59	65	63
No Parliament	9	14	10	11
N	1482	1508	1508	1854
Three-option referendum				
Independence	–	–	24	24
More powers	–	–	43	38
Status quo	–	–	33	38
N			1330	1558
SNP % regional vote	27	21	31	44

Sources: Scottish Social Attitudes 1999–2007; SES 2007 post-election survey; SES 2011 pre- and post-election surveys.

Parliament with its existing powers'), further devolution ('Give the Scottish Parliament power over all domestic matters including taxes and spending'), and independence ('Make Scotland an independent state within the European Union'). This question was asked in 2007 and 2011 but, in the earlier version, the middle option was more vaguely worded as 'Keep the Scottish Parliament but give it greater powers' while in the 2011 version fiscal control was mentioned explicitly. By 2011 fiscal autonomy had become a more central part of elite political debates (though whether these debates were appreciated by the public is unclear) and may explain why 'more powers' lost support to the 'status quo' option between the two elections. However, it is clear that, regardless of the measure used, support for independence barely changed between 2007 and 2011 and indeed since devolution (see Curtice et al. 2009: 57–59). This becomes even clearer when we also consider the SNP's share of the regional list vote at each election. The stasis in support for independence compared with the large fluctuations in vote shares shows clearly that the former cannot explain the latter.

There is no paradox in the fact that SNP support has more than doubled between 2003 and 2011 while support for independence has flatlined. It simply means that other factors drove the party's vote share. That conclusion is consistent with evidence, accumulated from a series of surveys of the Scottish electorate, that constitutional preferences are an important influence on party choice but are far from the whole story (Paterson et al. 2001: ch. 4; Bromley et al. 2006: ch. 4; Johns et al. 2010: ch. 10). Voters can and do distinguish between choosing Scotland's government and choosing Scotland's constitutional future. As emphasized in this chapter, the SNP stood to gain from voters doing the former because of the positive evaluations of the SNP's record in office and scepticism about Labour's likely performance.

Next we use a structural model to test our thesis that the SNP gains are better explained by perceptions of competence than by constitutional preferences. For this, we turn to our panel of respondents who participated in both the 2007 and the 2011 election surveys in order to investigate the sources of opinion change between the two elections. All of the variables in this model have been introduced in previous analyses: the five-point national identity scale (see Table 2.4); self-placements on the 0–10 constitutional preference scale (Figure 4.1(ii)); SNP ratings on the 0–10 like/dislike scale (Table 3.3); and SNP competence evaluations via the assessment of its performance in office (Table 4.1).[5] Figure 4.2 presents the core results from estimating this model with the arrows being labelled with standardized path coefficients (betas or 'β's). A bold arrow indicates that that coefficient is statistically significantly different from zero.

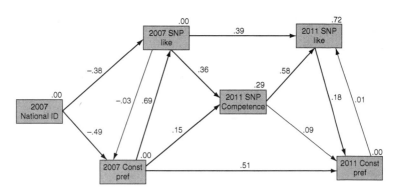

Figure 4.2 Structural model predicting attitudes to the SNP in 2011 ($N = 559$)
Source: SES panel (pre-election surveys), 2007–2011.

The 2007 variables serve as baselines for analysis. Not surprisingly, voters' attitudes to the SNP in 2007 were strongly influenced by their national identity and their constitutional preferences. Equally predictable is that those who liked the SNP in 2007 were, other things being equal, more likely to like the SNP in 2011 ($\beta = 0.39$) and that constitutional preference in 2007 was a powerful predictor of constitutional preference in 2011 ($\beta = 0.51$). The latter result further attests to the stability of constitutional attitudes between 2007 and 2011. More noteworthy is the fact that, once these 2007 variables are taken into account, constitutional preferences in 2011 have no significant influence on attitudes to the SNP in 2011. Voters were not won over to the SNP by its flagship policy of independence. Instead, the big driver of change in attitudes towards the SNP, that is, by far the most powerful influence once prior (2007) attitudes to the party are taken into account, was the competence evaluation ($\beta = 0.58$). Assessments of the SNP's record were themselves influenced by predispositions to like the party ($\beta = 0.36$) and to support its constitutional policy ($\beta = 0.15$), but these are influences and not determinants. Perceptions of the government's performance were formed to a considerable extent independently of prior SNP or independence sympathies, but then became a powerful influence on subsequent attitudes to the SNP.

As respondents' views on the constitutional question in 2011 were not perfectly predicted by respondents' views on the issue four years earlier, it is worth considering what else influenced the later preferences. It might have been thought that competence evaluations would have an impact: the stronger the performance of the Scottish government, the more likely voters would be to support independence or, at least, further devolution. There is some sign of a direct effect of competence on constitutional preferences but, at $\beta = 0.09$, it does not quite reach statistical significance. However, there is also an indirect effect of competence via attitudes to the SNP. Positive assessments of the government's performance generate support for the SNP and, in turn, boost support for its constitutional policy. The point should not be overstated: the indirect effect of competence on constitutional preferences amounts to the product of the two effects ($0.58 \times 0.18 = 0.10$) and, as such, is barely stronger than the direct effect. Nonetheless, this indirect effect highlights an interesting possibility, namely that it is not so much competent Scottish government in general but competent SNP government that makes people more willing to support constitutional change. All of this highlights one link between 'performance politics' and the constitutional issue. Constitutional preferences themselves have a valence dimension: that is, voters endorse the option that they deem most likely to deliver the desired outcomes. This was made clear as early as the 1997 devolution referendum (Brown et al. 1999, ch. 6; Denver et al. 2000: 159–168; see also Surridge 2006). Brown et al. summarize the point: 'Scots do not distinguish fundamentally between judging the effectiveness of policy and assessing the adequacy of the constitutional framework through which policy is made' (1999: 162). This echoes Fiorina's remark with which we opened this chapter. The constitutional issue is not so distinct from others. Though a minority of voters have strong views on constitutional politics, most simply care about what works.

There is another link between constitutional preferences and the specifically Scottish version of 'performance politics' that has been outlined in this chapter. The constitutional positions of interest here are not those of voters but those of the parties. We have emphasized the importance for parties of being seen to look after Scottish interests. It might reasonably be asked how voters determine whether a party 'looks after Scottish interests'. One means of judging this might be the parties' constitutional stances. Most agreed that the Conservatives' unpopularity in Scotland since the 1980s derived in part from opposition to devolution, not just because the majority of voters disagreed, but because it made the Conservatives appear anti-Scottish (Mitchell 1990; Brown et al. 1999: 89–90). Evidence from the 2007 SES indicated that Labour's perceived opposition to further devolution led voters to doubt the party's commitment to Scottish interests (Johns et al. 2010: 119–121). Here, we replicate that analysis using the 2011 data, calculating correlations between voters' placement of each party on the 0–10 constitution issue scale with their ratings of that party on Scottish interests. Positive correlations support the hypothesis that a party's willingness to support further devolution persuades voters of its concern for Scottish interests. In Table 4.9 the coefficients are shown for the full samples in 2007 and 2011, and then for each category of constitutional preference in 2011 as measured by the referendum question. We also show the mean placements of the parties in 2007 and 2011, useful

Table 4.9 Perceived constitutional stances and correlations with perceived commitment to Scottish interests, 2007 and 2011

	Conservative	Labour	Lib Dems	SNP	N (*min.*)
Mean placement on constitution scale					
2011	2.4	4.3	3.9	9.2	1618
2007	2.8	4.4	4.8	9.1	1479
Correlation with Scottish interests rating					
All voters – 2011	0.28	0.19	0.27	0.20	1301
All voters – 2007	0.09	0.19	0.19	0.16	1333
Status quo 2011	0.22	*0.04*	0.13	0.12	428
More powers 2011	0.28	0.21	0.37	0.12	455
Independence 2011	0.31	0.25	0.28	0.33	323

Note: The only correlation not significant at the *p* <0.05 level is italicized.
Sources: Pre-and post-election surveys.

contextual information given the argument that these perceptions are a means for judging commitment to Scottish interests.

Looking first at the results for all voters, we see that the correlations are all positive and statistically significant. Moreover, they are generally stronger in 2011 than in 2007, indicating that constitutional preferences have if anything become a more useful or, at least, a more widely used cue. This strengthening is clearest in the case of the two Westminster coalition parties, which is bad news for both as both were seen as having shifted their constitutional position towards the anti-devolution end of the scale (and thus away from the median voter's position on this issue). Labour got off more lightly but still suffered from voters' tendency to doubt its commitment to Scottish interests based on what they perceived as the party's continuing opposition to further devolution.

The breakdown by respondents' own constitutional preferences is instructive. It is not surprising that the correlations are generally strongest among those who themselves favour independence: this is naturally the group most likely to respond positively to parties that support substantial constitutional change. More telling are the positive correlations among the larger group favouring 'more powers', and the indications of at least some positive correlations among those favouring the status quo. In other words, voters do not have to share a party's support for further devolution or independence in order to give it credit for that stance if supporting further devolution or independence is seen as an indication of supporting Scottish interests even among opponents of these constitutional options. This may help explain why the SNP was credited almost universally with concern for Scottish interests, despite its policy of independence enjoying only minority support. In a situation where voters do not expect or particularly fear independence, it is easy to see how the indirect benefits of the party's constitutional stance could begin to stack up against the costs.

Conclusion

In the search for what is distinctive about Scottish Parliament elections, it is easy to overlook what is normal about them. The 2011 election was first and foremost about electing a party to govern Scotland. Even if a parliamentary majority for any party seemed highly unlikely, both of the leading contenders were perceived to be competing against each other for government office. Polls suggested that the electorate largely saw a choice between re-electing the SNP and replacing them with Labour. Our central argument in this chapter is that this choice helped the SNP for that most normal of reasons: most voters thought that the SNP was more competent to govern than its competitors, including its leading rival, the Labour Party. To explain the outcome of an election in one or two statistics is inevitably a crass exercise but the contrasting performance evaluations in Table 4.1 are a good place to start. To that extent, this is a straightforward case of 'performance politics'.

In concluding this chapter, we want to highlight a reason for the positive assessments of the SNP's term in office. The starting point is a contrast with 2007. At that election, voters were underwhelmed by Labour and had a relatively positive impression of the SNP and its leader. One reason for the very close race was that, because the SNP had no experience of government, voters were doubtful about the party's likely performance in government. Tabloid front pages on polling day in 2007 sought to play on such doubts, sketching apocalyptic scenarios in the event of an SNP victory, and many commentators expected the party's first experience of government to come to an abrupt end long before 2011. Since then, of course, much of the uncertainty about the SNP as a party of government has dissipated. This notion of the SNP easing voters' doubts is particularly applicable to the constitutional issue. Principally via its commitment to a referendum, the party sought to reassure voters that the election of an SNP government would not lead inevitably to independence. On the contrary, during the 2007–2011 term, the SNP focused instead on developing the kind of valence credentials – competence, financial credibility, strong leadership – that we have argued were crucial to its electoral gains. The SNP's case for re-election may have been further helped by the economic crisis, which, for most voters, became a more immediate concern than the constitutional question. The SNP appeared competent in government, dealing with the economic and fiscal crisis and the resultant UK government's strategy of fiscal retrenchment. The second point highlights the specifically Scottish dimension to 'performance politics' in this context: prospective governments are judged by their capacity not just to govern competently but to do so in a manner that defends Scotland's interests. Of course, none of this is to say that the constitutional question was irrelevant in this election. As we will see in the full models in Chapter 6, it remains quite a powerful predictor of party choice, and there remains a substantial group of voters who are strongly opposed to independence and are worried enough at the prospect to vote accordingly, just as there is an element that is strongly in favour of independence.

5
How 'Scottish' Was this Election?

From before the first devolved contest in 1999, there have been concerns about the extent to which Scottish voters would use Holyrood elections to focus on the stuff of domestic politics, and to hold the Scottish government accountable, rather than to pass comment on the performance of the Westminster government or to express their views on recent or future constitutional change. In the terms introduced in the opening chapter, the question was whether these were first- or second-order elections (Reif and Schmitt 1980). We also noted in Chapter 1 that subsequent work has long since refined that simple dichotomy, instead positing a continuum from purely second order to purely first order. In this context, the second-order extreme of that continuum would be a Scottish election entirely driven by events and personalities at Westminster, while the first-order extreme would be one in which politics at the UK level was entirely irrelevant and voters chose purely according to what was going on at Holyrood. Put simply, the question concerns the 'Scottishness' of this election.

Borrowing from the scale conventionally used (including in Chapter 2 of this book) to measure national identity, Denver and Johns (2010) characterized the 2007 election as 'More Scottish than British' – that is, closer to the first- than to the second-order end of the continuum sketched above. It was also appreciably more Scottish than the first two devolved contests. Voting in those elections, as described by Paterson et al. (2001) and Curtice (2006), was considerably influenced by evaluations of the UK government but, even more so, by attitudes to devolution itself. In both elections, party choice reflected above all voters' attitudes towards the Parliament and towards the possibility of further constitutional change, and seemed to have rather little to do with goings on at Holyrood.

There is an obvious reason why 2007 was a more Scottish election. Devolution had had another four years to bed in and so the elected Scottish government was a more familiar, a more powerful and a more prominent player. For the same reasons, we would expect the 2011 election to be still more Scottish – that is, to fall closer to the first-order end of the continuum. The impact of the Scottish government's policies and performance on the average voter is strengthening with each election. Moreover, the devolved arena is the focus of considerable media attention. Coverage such as the televising of First Minister's Questions is a specific example of a more general commitment to cover Scotland not just as a region with distinctive attitudes and reactions to Westminster politics but as a polity in itself. In sum, devolution has enhanced a Scottish political arena that, though sharing reciprocal influence with Westminster's events and personalities, is increasingly distinct from the UK political arena. Scottish voters inhabit two political worlds (Blake et al. 1985).

Adopting this notion of two worlds, or two parallel arenas, the relevance of the first- to second-order model of elections becomes more questionable. We have already noted in Chapter 1 that Scotland's semi-proportional electoral system and distinct party system thus make it difficult to assess the 'order' of Scottish Parliament elections (Reif and Schmitt 1980). Holyrood and Westminster are not simply two alternative arenas in which the same politics are played out. The rules, the players, and above all the relative strength of those players are all quite different. The SNP did not edge the 2007 election because they were a suitable channel for protest voting against Labour's record at the UK level. It was because, in a Scottish-only election, the SNP becomes a viable contender for office and was marginally preferred to a Labour-led Scottish government whose record left voters generally unimpressed (Johns et al. 2010).

There is another reason why, if we think of Scottish elections as taking place in a distinct political arena, assessing whether these are first order, second order or something in between may be to address the wrong question. The notion of the 'order' of an election gives primacy to relative importance – how much voters see at stake in these elections compared with those to Westminster or to local councils.

This question, however, fails to consider that the 'Scottishness' of Scottish elections is probably at least as much a function of absolute importance. That is, a voter who thought there was much at stake in the 2011 Scottish election, and therefore cared who won, could be expected to vote based on Scottish matters. It would not matter that there had been a Westminster election in 2010 in which the same voter believed there was even more at stake. What matters is the significance attributed by voters to what goes on in the Scottish political world at the time of the Scottish elections.

What voters see at stake in Scottish elections

A first empirical look at this question of perceived importance comes from a long-established survey question asking respondents: 'How much of a difference do you think it makes who wins in elections: (i) to the Scottish Parliament? (ii) to the UK House of Commons? In previous surveys, Westminster elections have been seen as making slightly more difference than Holyrood elections (Curtice 2006; Johns et al. 2010). By 2011, that gap narrowed so that there was not a significant difference in the perceived relative importance of the elections. In both cases, about half of the respondents (51.5 per cent for Westminster, 50 per cent for Holyrood) declared that the elections in question made 'a great deal' of difference. Only 7 per cent of respondents (down from 11 per cent in 2007) thought that Scottish election outcomes made 'not very much' or 'no difference at all'. These results may exaggerate voters' interest: by asking a long series of questions about elections, we make it harder for a respondent to report indifference to their outcomes. Nonetheless, the results from this question are consistent with our argument that Scottish elections are regarded as important in absolute as well as relative terms.

This leads to the questions: *why* do voters think it matters who wins Scottish elections? What do they think *is* at stake? One answer to these questions lies in voters' attributions of responsibility: that is, the extent to which they see the Scottish government as responsible for key policy areas. SES respondents were asked: 'Thinking about the Scottish and UK governments, which do you think is mainly responsible for the following issue areas?' Four areas – law and order, health, education and the economy – were asked about

Table 5.1 Percentage deeming each level 'mainly responsible' for
key policy areas, 2007–2011

		Scottish	UK	Don't know	N
Law & order	2007	50	39	11	1872
	2011	57	34	9	1756
Health	2007	59	31	10	1872
	2011	68	24	8	1756
Education	2007	70	20	10	1872
	2011	74	18	8	1756
Economy	2007	26	60	14	1552
	2011	10	82	8	1756

Sources: SES 2007 pre- and post-election surveys; SES 2011 post-election
survey.

in both the 2007 and 2011 surveys and responses from both years
are presented in Table 5.1. The results suggest a growing tendency
to attribute responsibility to one or other level of government while
the proportion of 'don't know' responses fell on each issue. More
significantly, in all four cases there was a move towards consensus.
On the economy, this meant a substantial proportion believing that
the UK government was mainly responsible for economic policy.
However, with the other three issues, growing proportions believed
that devolution leaves them mainly the province of the government
in Edinburgh.

Law and order, health and education encompass many of voters' most pressing everyday concerns. Indeed, as Table 4.4 shows,
each had been reported by significant proportions of voters as their
'most important issue' when deciding how to vote in the 2007 election. So there is at the very least the potential for voters to see
much at stake in Scottish elections. However, as the same table
shows, those issues were hugely overshadowed by the economy in
2011. If economic responsibility was overwhelmingly attributed to
the UK government, then we might expect 2011 to have reversed the
trend towards 'first-order' status for Scottish elections. At first
glance, it looks as if many voters reported basing their choice on
an issue they thought the government up for election could do little about. On this reading, the context of the 2011 election made it

a multi-level contest in which the more economically powerful level was inevitably dominant. However, we cannot conclude from Table 5.1 that economic voting in 2011 was inevitably a second-order commentary on developments at Westminster. Two aspects of the survey question involved mean that such a conclusion would be premature. The first, echoing a point made earlier, is that it is a relative rather than an absolute measure. Respondents might concede that Westminster is *mainly* responsible for economic policy but nonetheless also see the Scottish government as having some responsibility for this. Secondly, there is an important distinction between responsibility for policy (or *functional* responsibility) and responsibility for outcomes (or *causal* responsibility). Governments are functionally responsible for those policy domains constitutionally assigned to them; they are causally responsible for the outcomes that result from their actions (Brickman et al. 1982; Iyengar 1989). Admittedly, this distinction should not be overdrawn. In politics, as Arceneaux (2006: 736) points out, 'outcomes are often complex and the product of multiple causes. Voters need only believe that government policy could have done more to avert a problem even if it was caused by something else'. On this reading, a government could be deemed causally responsible for an outcome if it holds the powers – the functional responsibility – to have done something about that outcome. Nonetheless, it is worth considering whether voters distinguish between policy outcomes and responsibility for those outcomes.

That may be achieved by returning to the questions initially analysed in Tables 4.2 and 4.3 in the previous chapter. Having reported their assessment of outcomes in four policy areas, respondents were asked whether this was mainly the result of the policies of the UK government at Westminster, the policies of the Scottish government, both equally or some other reason. The results are shown in Table 5.2. On each of the four issues, the picture is less clear-cut than Table 5.1 implies. This is not surprising. Quite apart from the difficulties in partitioning responsibility between Westminster and Holyrood, both levels are at the mercy of external circumstances: demographic trends, global economic conditions, the choices of previous governments (see Chapter 1 for discussion). The relatively large percentages of 'don't knows' are therefore unsurprising. Among those who did respond, there is a clear and consistent pattern on the first three issues. Citizens recognize the Scottish government's greater

Table 5.2 Percentage deeming each level 'mainly responsible' for outcomes since 2007

	Law and order %	Health %	Education %	Living standards %
Scottish government	38	41	40	21
UK government	10	11	9	32
Both equally	28	27	22	29
Some other reason	5	4	3	7
Don't know	20	17	26	12
N	1760	1760	1760	1760

Source: SES 2011 post-election survey.

influence in these devolved areas but many assign at least some responsibility to the UK government. The considerable proportions opting for 'both equally' might reflect uncertainty or might reflect a recognition that 'in devolved policy domains' Holyrood's scope for action is influenced by Westminster's budgetary policies.

There is a similar pattern in reverse on the living standards question. The overall balance of responses reflects the view that Westminster is more often deemed responsible though fully 50 per cent of respondents assign equal or primary responsibility to Holyrood. This is likely to be at least partly due to the use of 'living standards' rather than 'the economy' in the question. It makes sense that the Scottish government (not least due to its responsibility for policies that influence public health, education, welfare and well-being) would have more influence over the broader matter of living standards than over the economy in particular. Nonetheless, the results suggest that devolved affairs will have contributed to shaping economic evaluations and expectations in 2011. The point is reinforced by a separate question, cast in absolute rather than relative terms, asking respondents: 'How much do you think the Scottish government's policies influence the overall performance of Scotland's economy?' Fully 77 per cent of respondents (cf 53 per cent in 2007) credited the Scottish government with 'a great deal' or a 'fair amount' of influence, opening up the possibility that there was a multi-level dimension not only to voting in general in 2011 but, in particular, to voting on the key issue of the economy.

The economy in multi-level context

To examine that possibility more closely, we use a multi-level measure of issue importance. In the previous chapter, we reported on an open-ended question asking respondents in the post-election survey to name the issue most important to them when deciding how to vote. Here, we turn to pre-election survey questions asking respondents about the most important issues facing Britain and Scotland. Specifically, respondents were asked: 'As far as you're concerned, what is the *single most important issue* facing Britain at the present time?' Then: 'And what is the *single most important issue* facing Scotland at the present time?' As Table 5.3 shows, the two questions elicited similar response patterns. This reflects the importance of economic issues in 2011 though the dominance of the economy in both cases is notable given that the questions were designed to encourage differentiation. Having reported an issue (in many cases the economy) facing

Table 5.3 Most important issue facing: (i) Britain (ii) Scotland

	Britain %	Scotland %
Economy	44	34
Public finances	12	10
Immigration	12	4
Unemployment	10	20
Terrorism	2	0
Defence	2	0
Crime	2	4
Health	2	2
Inequality	2	1
Energy	1	2
Independence	1	9
Welfare	1	1
Education	1	1
Alcohol/Drugs	0	2
Political	3	4
Other	5	5
N	916	1134

Source: SES pre-election survey.

Britain in general, respondents were then invited to consider whether a different issue faced Scotland more specifically. There was some evidence of a distinction between levels in that many respondents named 'the economy' in general to the first question and cited unemployment as the particular economic problem confronting Scotland. However, the overall result is clear and consistent across both questions: if concerns about the public finances are included, around two-thirds of respondents saw economic issues as the most important facing Britain and Scotland.[1]

This does not in itself demonstrate a multi-level economic vote in 2011. Respondents may have seen economic problems as the most pressing issue facing Scotland but, at the same time, believed that only the Westminster government – or that neither level of government – could do anything about these problems. However, a more interesting pattern than that emerges when we look at the results from the same follow-up question about party competence that formed the basis for Table 4.5 in the previous chapter. After the 'most important issue' question for each level, respondents were asked to name the party that they regarded as best able to handle that issue. In Table 5.4, we show the results for those naming either the economy (a broad category also including references to 'the financial crisis') or unemployment. To make the distribution among the parties clearer, we exclude the roughly 20 per cent in each case who answered 'don't know' when asked which party would handle these issues best.

The results highlight the multi-level nature of economic evaluations in 2011. When respondents thought about the economic problems facing Britain, they were likeliest to name Labour as best

Table 5.4 Party best able to handle economic issues facing Britain and Scotland (row percentages)

		None	Con	Lab	LD	SNP	Other	N
Britain	Economy	18	25	34	3	18	2	594
	Unemployment	10	7	45	4	34	1	133
Scotland	Economy	13	8	28	3	47	1	478
	Unemployment	11	4	33	3	48	1	267

Source: Pre-election survey.

equipped to deal with them, with the Conservatives also given some credit (for handling the economy if not unemployment). However, when respondents – in many cases the *same* respondents – considered the economic and employment situation in Scotland, comfortably the largest proportion named the SNP as best able to handle these problems. In the previous chapter, we highlighted the SNP's lead in terms of economic competence as an important plank in their electoral success. Now we can see why that advantage was so important. Had the economy simply been a Westminster issue intruding on a Holyrood election, then the SNP's perceived competence would have mattered little and, presumably, Labour would have stood to benefit – as it had in the general election the previous year. The SNP was credited with influence over the nation's economy, and voters tended to think the SNP best equipped to exert that influence.

The point about a 'multi-level economic vote' is reinforced by comparing respondents' pre-election reports of the most important issues facing Britain and Scotland with their post-election reports of the most important issue in their voting decision. There was surprisingly little consistency between the two: it seems that 'objective' assessments of the country's priorities play only a limited role in driving personal vote choices. For example, only around two in five of those who said that the economy or employment was the most important problem facing the country then cited either of those issues as the primary motivation behind their party choice. The key point for present purposes, however, is that that proportion was basically the same, regardless of whether the country in question was Britain (41 per cent) or Scotland (42 per cent).[2] In other words, economic voting was no less common among those whose principal focus was on the Scottish level. While some voters were choosing between the alternative economic strategies proposed by the two main rivals at Westminster, plenty of others were assessing how the Scottish economy would fare under the leading contenders for government at Holyrood.

The basis for decision-making: Voters' self-reports

The same argument – that some voters focus principally on UK politics while others' decisions are based on the Scottish level – applies not only to the economy but to electoral choice in general. What is difficult is to determine is the relative importance of the different levels: that is, which drives more voting decisions? There are, broadly speaking, two ways of addressing this question. One is to use the kinds of multivariate models of party choice reported in previous chapters and to examine whether the more powerful predictors of party choice have more to do with UK or with Scottish politics. For example, in Chapter 3 we showed that attitudes to the Scottish party leaders had more influence over party choice than did attitudes to the Westminster leaders. We return to such comparisons in the next chapter when reporting our full models of party choice in 2011. Here, we use the second approach to determining the relative importance of arenas – that is, simply asking voters. This direct approach has its limitations. The title of Timothy D. Wilson's (2004) *Strangers to Ourselves* encapsulates the central message of his psychological research, that people seldom have a clear idea of what drives their decisions. This is why political scientists have rarely paid much heed to respondents' own accounts of why they voted a certain way – such reports are unreliable and often consist of rationalizations rather than true reasons. However, unreliability need not imply bias. There is no obvious reason why limits on introspective access would lead respondents to overstate the impact of either the Scottish or the British level on their voting decision. So, while we might be sceptical about any given individual's reported reasons for their vote, the aggregated results from our sample may still be informative.

In surveys at all four Scottish elections, those who reported voting were asked whether, in choosing their party, they had in mind mostly what was going on in Scotland or mostly what was going on in Britain as a whole (Curtice 2006: 93).[3] The top panel of Table 5.5 shows that, throughout this period, a clear majority of voters have reported deciding primarily on Scottish matters. The proportion had looked to be rising steadily as devolution bedded in, giving Scottish Parliament elections an increasingly first-order character, but that trend levelled off in 2011. This could reflect a kind of 'ceiling effect', whereby the continuing importance of Westminster in Scottish politics means that the proportion is unlikely to rise much above 70 per cent. However, it might instead reflect only a temporary interruption of the upward trend, due perhaps to the importance of the economy in 2011. This will be best resolved by surveys at future elections. In the meantime, some light can be shed on the matter by looking at

Table 5.5　Basis for voting decision, 1999–2011, and by selected 'most important issue' in 2011

	Mostly Scotland	Mostly Britain	N
All voters			
1999	62	38	878
2003	67	33	736
2007	71	29	1091
2011	70	30	1367
2011 by 'most important issue'			
Economy/jobs	67	33	327
Education/health	76	24	82
Constitution	65	35	140
Parties/leaders	65	35	139
No issue mentioned	69	31	331

Note: This question was asked only of those who reported voting in that election.
Sources: SSA (1999, 2003); SES post-election surveys (2007, 2011).

responses to the Scottish/British question by reported 'most important issue' when voting. Rather than taking up the space required for a full breakdown, we focus in the bottom panel of Table 5.5 on the most common issue responses.

The breakdown by most important issue reinforces the central message from the previous section: economic voting in 2011 was by no means just a second-order reaction to the British government's economic management. Those citing the economy as the most important issue in their decision split in roughly the same way as the electorate as a whole in reporting their focus when voting. This exemplifies the more general point that Table 5.5 shows little sign of the kind of differences that we might expect given the constitutional arrangements. Those concerned with education and health were a little more likely to report focusing on the devolved level, but the main theme is homogeneity. One could argue that this better reflects the constitutional reality, whereby almost any issue has both British and Scottish dimensions. In that case, what Table 5.5 tells us is less about voters' attributions of responsibility and more about their focus of interest. A substantial minority described their 2011 vote as a response to what was going on in British politics. Whatever their issue priorities, most voters were focused principally on the Scottish arena.[4] Questions about the basis for voters' choices have typically been asked in the context of discussions about the *status*, rather than about the *outcomes*, of Scottish Parliament elections. Yet, in 2011 in particular, there is good reason to suppose that the result – or, at least, the margin of victory – depended on whether voters' main focus was on British or Scottish politics.

Labour's best hope of replicating its success in 2010 was by encouraging a referendum on the Westminster government; the SNP preferred a 'domestic valence' competition in order to maximize profits from its competence advantage over Scottish Labour. Table 5.4 has already illustrated the point in the economic context: voters thinking about Britain's problems tended to see Labour as best equipped to handle the issue, while those focused on the Scottish economy favoured the SNP. In Table 5.6, we look more directly at voting behaviour, investigating for both 2011 and 2007 how regional vote choice varied by reported basis for choice.

Looking first at the 2011 results, we see clear confirmation of the (hardly startling) hypothesis that party choice differs according to the political arena on which voters are focusing. The SNP is the majority choice among those deciding mostly according to what was going on in Scotland. Labour trails by fully 31 points in that category – which,

Table 5.6   Regional list vote by reported main focus, 2011 and 2007

	2011		2007	
	Scotland %	Britain %	Scotland %	Britain %
Conservative	9	20	11	21
Labour	22	37	27	34
Lib Dem	6	3	10	12
SNP	53	27	37	19
Other	12	11	14	15
N	941	410	748	324

Note: The data are weighted by actual vote shares so that comparison is not distorted by any changes in sampling or non-response bias.
Source: SES post-election surveys, 2007 and 2011.

as we saw earlier, contains more than two thirds of those who voted. By contrast, when we consider those focused principally on the British level, Labour has a ten-point lead over the SNP and the Conservatives enjoy at least a relatively strong showing. (Leaving aside the predictable collapse in the Liberal Democrat percentage, these results are at least somewhat reminiscent of the 2010 general election results in Scotland.) It is not difficult to see why Labour and the SNP went into the 2011 campaign wanting the election to be fought on very different territory.

However, the comparison with 2007 adds nuance to that conclusion. The election of a Conservative-led government at Westminster did not lead to a marked improvement in Labour's showing among those focused on that British level; if anything, it is the SNP that advanced most among that group to become clearly the second party. So, while it made sense for Labour in 2011 to try to focus voters' attention on Westminster rather than Holyrood, the party would have had to be spectacularly successful in that regard – far more so than looks remotely likely given the trend shown in Table 5.5 – in order to deliver victory. Labour's advantage over the SNP among British-focused voters was relatively narrow and certainly dwarfed by its disadvantage among the Scottish-focused. Put another way, while the SNP's landslide was owed primarily to its huge lead among that latter group it was also enabled by the party's ability to win significant numbers of votes from those focused on British politics. This echoes conclusions from earlier in this book about the broad base of the SNP's gains. Headway was made in all groups, even – or especially – among those hitherto harder for the party to reach.

That last point should not obscure the clear comparative advantages shown in Table 5.6. In 2007 and 2011, Labour was clearly preferred among those basing their choice on British politics and the SNP clearly preferred among those instead concerned with the Scottish level. The differences are sufficiently large that we can not only speak of different political worlds but say that, within Scotland, the British and Scottish political worlds have different party systems. The former resembles the British party system as a whole but with the familiar differences: Labour stronger, the Conservatives weaker, and a strong SNP presence. The latter is very different, with two-party competition between the currently dominant SNP and Labour and the others playing only a minor role. In the final section of this chapter, we examine whether these different party systems are reflected in different patterns of party allegiances when voters are prompted to distinguish these two political worlds.

Multi-level party support

The multi-level context that has developed under devolution has, as we have already pointed out, complicated how we think of party support and vote choice in Scotland. With the creation and expansion of multiple levels of government in what was the model unitary system, we can expect that the party systems in the nations (Scotland, Wales and Northern Ireland) would take on unique characteristics specific to those systems (Dunleavy 2005). One way to examine the extent to which devolution has reshaped the party system in Scotland is to look at the patterns of partisan attachments within the Scottish electorate. The question addressed in this section, then, is whether, in line with the different incentives, incumbents and incidents in the Westminster and Holyrood arenas, the Scots have also developed distinct partisan attachments across these contexts. We know that voting patterns differ substantially across the two arenas; here, we consider whether it is not just short-term behaviour but also long-term partisan allegiances that varies. Are these allegiances contingent on the arena that voters are thinking about at the time?

Repeated analyses (Clarke et al. 2004; Johns et al. 2010) have demonstrated that many voters still broadly 'identify' with parties and that these identities or affiliations matter – and matter substantially – in predicting vote choice. However, party identification is decreasing across most established democracies (Dalton 2006; Scarrow 2000; Whiteley 2009) and some parties are disproportionately feeling the effects of de-alignment (Dunleavy 2005). And, as noted in Chapter 3, many scholars have questioned whether we should really discuss party identification as a longstanding allegiance or instead think of it as a more ephemeral preference (Fiorina 1981; Burden and Klofstad 2005; Johnston 2006). Panel studies using the British Election Study surveys have shown that around two-thirds of those who report a party allegiance maintain a consistent identification with that same political party. That leaves a substantial group that switches not only vote but also reported allegiance between elections – sometimes more than once (Clarke and Stewart 1998: 371;

but see Dunleavy 2005: 511). This transience or flexibility is highly relevant for our question about the possibility of parallel identifications across political arenas. If party identification conforms simply to the Michigan model, with most voters socialized in early life into a strong emotional bond with a party, we would expect not only stability in partisanship but also consistency across the Scottish and British political arenas. Such party loyalties would not be so conditional.

However, if partisan attitudes are more ephemeral, driven by short-term factors like performance, policies and personalities, then we might well expect reported party identification to differ across arenas insofar as the parties have experienced contrasting fortunes at Westminster and Holyrood.

While there are several different ways that we could go about priming respondents to consider different levels of government and then observing any impact on their party attachments, in this instance we opted for the most straightforward prime – we instructed respondents directly to think about the different arenas. At the beginning of the second, or post-election, wave of the SES, we embedded a simple survey experiment prompting respondents to consider their partisan allegiances at different levels of government. Respondents were asked two sets of questions, one about their party preference at the UK (Westminster) level and the other about their preference at the Scottish (Holyrood) level. These were worded as follows:

Some people think of themselves as usually being a supporter of one political party rather than another (even if they might vote for a different party from time to time). Thinking about *UK politics at Westminster*, do you usually think of yourself as being a supporter of one particular party or not?

Thinking now about *Scottish politics at Holyrood*, do you usually think of yourself as being a supporter of one particular party or not?

In either case, those who answered 'Yes, I do' were then asked:

Which Party is that?
Labour
Conservative

Liberal Democrat
Scottish National Party
Green Party
Other [write in option]

It is well established that responses to survey questions can be shaped by the context set by previous questions (Schuman and Presser 1996, ch. 2). It is possible, for example, that asking first about respondent party preferences at the UK level would put that context into respondents' minds in a way that persisted despite the fact that the next question specifically mentions Holyrood. Another possibility is that respondents might wish to appear consistent in their preferences, or to avoid appearing 'disloyal' to the party that they named first. All of these biases would artificially inflate the observed level of partisan consistency across arenas, and all of them imply that responses to the second question are somehow contaminated. We therefore randomly assigned half of the SES respondents to receive first the UK question followed by the Scotland question, while the other half of respondents were first asked about Scottish politics, then UK. Put another way, the order of the two questions above was switched between our two randomly assigned groups of respondents.

Table 5.7 presents the basic response patterns for the two sets of multi-level party identification questions. On the left, under 'Split Half 1', is the series that first asks respondents to report their party preference at the UK level, then at the Scottish level. The two columns on the right ('Split Half 2') present the percentages of respondents identifying with the parties (or not) when we first ask about the Scottish level, then the UK. Two basic patterns are evident with these responses. First, there is a great deal of aggregate stability in the percentages of people saying that they do not think of themselves as supporting the parties at both levels no matter whether they are first primed to think about Scotland or the UK. Similarly, the percentages of respondents saying that they support the smaller Scottish parties (the Liberal Democrats, Greens and 'Others') are stable no matter whether they are prompted to first think about Holyrood or Westminster.

On the other hand, Table 5.7 also reveals some slight evidence of shifting between Labour and SNP support depending on the order of consideration. SNP support is slightly stronger when respondents

Table 5.7 Responses to multi-level party identification questions, column percentages

	Split half 1		Split half 2	
	UK (asked first)	Scotland (asked second)	Scotland (asked first)	UK (asked second)
None	40%	38%	36%	40%
Conservative	13	8	9	13
Labour	23	16	21	27
Lib Dem	4	3	4	5
SNP	19	33	30	13
Green	1	1	1	0
Other	1	1	1	2
N	896	896	867	867

are first primed to think about the UK level. That is, comparing the SNP support across the two halves of the sample, we find that the SNP fairs slightly better if respondents first consider the UK level, then the Scottish level. The opposite holds for Labour support. When respondents are asked to first consider the Scottish level, then the UK level, support for Labour improves slightly. In other words, asking first about the UK improves Labour identification (and suppresses SNP identification) at that level, but then somewhat suppresses Labour identification at the Scottish level (but improves SNP identification at that level). For both Labour and the SNP the shifts are noticeable, though not exactly earth-shattering (in the 3–6 percentage range).

The pattern revealed in the marginals immediately draws us to the question about shifting party support across the levels of governance. Tables 5.8 and 5.9 display SES respondents' Scottish and UK party support, conditional on the level they were first primed to consider. First we consider those respondents who were initially primed to think about the UK, then were asked about their Scottish party support (Table 5.8). Owing to the SNP being largely associated with Scotland, we could imagine that there might be some individuals who see themselves as SNP supporters within Scotland, but do not think much about a specific party at Westminster. Along these lines Table 5.8 shows that 18 per cent of those who say they do not support a party in Westminster (or 64 respondents) support the SNP in Scotland. Of course, one possibility here is that this is a survey

Table 5.8 Scottish party identification conditional on UK party identification, column percentages

Scottish PID	UK PID (asked first)				
	None	Conservative	Labour	Lib Dem	SNP
None	**79**	21	14	14	0
Conservative	0	**60**	1	0	0
Labour	1	0	**66**	0	0
Lib Dem	1	2	0	**71**	0
SNP	18	18	19	9	**100**
Green	0	0	0	6	0
Other	0	0	0	0	0
N	356	114	209	35	168

Table 5.9 UK party identification conditional on Scottish party identification, column percentages

UK PID	Scottish PID (asked first)				
	None	Conservative	Labour	Lib Dem	SNP
None	**78**	3	4	6	35
Conservative	8	**97**	0	3	5
Labour	9	0	**96**	0	13
Lib Dem	3	0	0	**91**	2
SNP	0	0	0	0	**43**
Green	0	0	0	0	0
Other	1	0	0	0	2
N	309	74	178	32	262

'artefact' that is the result of the Scottish question falling second in the sequence. Some relatively small percentage of respondents may have thought that, not having specified a party at the UK level, they should specify a party at the Scottish level to avoid looking completely apolitical. And there is some evidence of this – of the 64 respondents in the second wave who said they did not support a party in Westminster but supported the SNP in Scotland, 44 of them said that they were non-partisans in the SES' first wave while just 16 said that they supported the SNP. On the other hand, we do not see a similar pattern when we reverse the order of the UK and Scottish questions.

Turning to respondents who specified a party at the UK level, the broad pattern is that those respondents also generally report supporting the same party in Scotland: 60 per cent of UK Conservatives, 66 per cent of UK Labour and 71 per cent of Liberal Democrats said that they supported the same party when primed to consider Scottish politics.

At the same time, non-trivial percentages of UK partisans seemed to be hard-pressed to declare a party at the Scottish level and, not surprisingly, this problem seemed to afflict the UK Conservative identifiers (21 per cent) more so than the UK Labour (14 per cent) or UK Liberal Democrats (14 per cent). Of course, what we are particularly intrigued by are those people who report party switching. Consistently across the parties, the main beneficiary of party switching between levels of government was the SNP: 18 per cent of Conservatives, 19 per cent of Labour and 9 per cent of Liberal Democrats said that when they thought about Scottish politics, they were inclined to support the SNP. (As a side note, we would point out that the slightly lower percentage of Liberal Democrat 'switchers' is likely owing to the phenomenon we have mentioned throughout this book – the collapse of the Liberal Democrat support generally means that by the time of our survey only the 'hardcore' supporters declared fealty to the Liberal Democrats, thus we are less likely to find Liberal Democrat 'switchers'.)

So far we have not mentioned the UK SNP supporters. Not surprisingly, all (100 per cent) of respondents who said they support the SNP at the UK level went on to declare support for the same party at the Scottish level. A similar pattern is apparent in Table 5.9, which reports respondent UK party support for the other half of the sample of respondents (first asked about their Scottish party support). Here the overwhelming pattern is that those respondents who declared support for Scottish Conservatives, Scottish Labour and Scottish Liberal Democrats consistently supported the same party at the UK level. What seems to be important to determining the consistency of party support across the UK and Scottish levels of government is the main arena of political conflict as perceived by the individual. For example, respondents who consistently support the SNP at the UK level tend to see the outcome of the Scottish Parliament elections as being

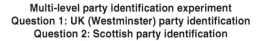

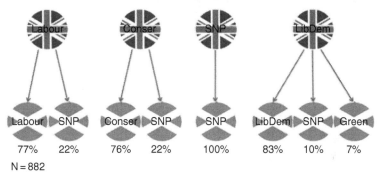

77% 22% 76% 22% 100% 83% 10% 7%

N = 882

Figure 5.1 Multi-level party identification experiment

Multi-level party identification experiment
Question 1: Scottish party identification
Question 2: UK (Westminster) party identification

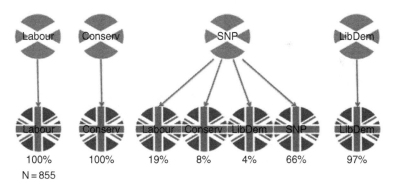

100% 100% 19% 8% 4% 66% 97%

N = 855

Figure 5.2 Multi-level party identification experiment

far more important (mean = 1.2) than do consistent supporters of the Conservatives and Labour (means = 1.9 and 1.8, respectively).

These patterns are perhaps a bit easier to discern in Figures 5.1 and 5.2. Excluding non-partisans, these figures show the patterns of party switching depending on the order (UK or Scotland) in which we primed respondents to think about their party support. Figure 5.1

shows the 'Scottish-centric' nature of those supporters who consistently support the SNP. Of interest also is the fact that the SNP is the main (and, indeed in the case of Labour and Conservative, only) beneficiary of switching from the UK to the Scottish level. Figure 5.2 shows that Scottish Labour and Conservative (and almost all Scottish Liberal Democrats) consistently support the same party at the UK level, while in that other arena of conflict, SNP supporters split between the parties (with almost 20 per cent of support going to UK Labour).

What do these patterns mean for 'real world' political competition? We would posit, as mentioned above, that the relative success (or not) of the parties' election campaigns in the General and Scottish elections has a great deal to do with their assumed pattern of party support. In 2011 Scottish Labour ran what we and many others have identified as a Westminster-focused campaign, basing their campaign on an implicit model of party support wherein Scottish Labour could count on the votes of those people who just voted for Scottish Labour candidates in the previous year's general election. But the SES data reveal that when priming the different political arenas, different patterns of party support, and therefore vote choice, emerge (Table 5.10).

A final point to address with our experiment in multi-level party support is how the questions priming different governing levels compare to the standard, non-level specific party support measure. As noted above, in addition to our post-election party support experiment, the SES asked the standard party support question in the pre-election wave. Table 5.10 presents a comparison between the questions priming the Scottish and UK levels with the pre-election party support question. Here, we simply combined the responses

Table 5.10 Party support combining post-election experimental halves, row percentages

	Conservative	Labour	Lib Dem	SNP	Green	Other	No party	N
Scotland(%)	8	18	4	32	1	1	37	1763
UK(%)	13	25	4	16	0	1	40	1763
Pre-election(%)	9	20	4	19	0	1	46	2046

from the two-halves to create single party support measures for the different levels.[5] It appears that the aggregated response pattern to the general party support measure used in most surveys in Scotland is something of a rough 'average' of the Scottish and UK party support measures. Looking specifically at Conservative and Labour support, the pre-election measure falls right in between the Scottish and UK measures while SNP support comes in at somewhat below the 'average' of the two. Further, the general measure seems to elicit – at least in the case of the 2011 SES – a higher percentage of non-identifiers. Clearly, the level of government under consideration when survey respondents report their party support matters a great deal. At the same time, we would emphasize the usual caveats when drawing conclusions from cross-sectional survey evidence. To use the standard cliché, cross-sectional surveys provide a 'snapshot in time' that draws on one particular sample of respondents. To understand how robust these results are, we will have to replicate this experiment in future surveys.

Conclusion: 'More Scottish than British'

Scottish governance involves an increasingly complex set of arrangements that share power for devolved policy domains across Scottish and UK institutions. In that sense, no Scottish election is isolated from British politics and no UK election in Scotland is isolated from Scottish politics. Yet the very complexity of those arrangements is such that we cannot expect a voter to pay much heed to them when making his or her decision. There is mounting evidence that voters, while they may have a reasonably clear idea of how formal policy responsibilities are shared among different levels of government (see Table 5.1), do not take account of these attributions when voting (Anderson 2006; Cutler 2004: 34–35; Arceneaux 2006; Johns 2011; León 2011). The simplest explanation for this is that voters lack the motivation to consider constitutional niceties when making a choice. Rather, they are more passive consumers. If an issue is prominent during an election campaign, it is likely to influence voting decisions regardless of whether it is, in strictly constitutional terms, 'at stake' in that election.

Broadening this from specific issues to the importance of over-all arenas – that is, to the question of the 'Scottishness' of this election – we find drawbacks in the 'order of elections' approach that has dominated research in this area. In that model, voters are pictured as cognitively active, calculating the relative importance of the level to be elected. More likely is that they are passive, responding to the way that Scottish election campaigns are presented to them by the parties and the media. If, during a Holyrood campaign, the media were preoccupied by events at Westminster and the parties in opposition at Westminster campaigned for a protest vote against the UK government, then we would not expect that election to be particularly Scottish. Conversely, a campaign focused on the devolved arena will generate a Scottish election, regardless of the fact that the Westminster government might be more powerful. This is why we have emphasized the idea of parallel political worlds or arenas, rather than the more commonly used term 'levels' of government. A horizontal is more apt than a vertical metaphor in a situation where what matters is not the relative importance of the body to be elected but the shifting focus of campaign attention.

Scottish elections have thus become more Scottish because devolution has carved out a distinct political arena within which these elections are conducted. The 2010 and 2011 elections yielded such starkly different results in Scotland because they were conducted in two different political worlds, each placing its own set of considerations and incentives before voters. The issue of the economy illustrates the point very well. While it was clearly the dominant concern in both elections, the nature of economic voting was conspicuously different across the two. In 2010, many voters rallied behind Labour in a bid to prevent a Conservative-led government taking office at Westminster. In 2011, voters could do nothing about the make-up of the UK government but they could elect the party at Holyrood that they deemed best able to defend Scotland against the effects of the coalition's fiscal tightening. The more powerful economic levers remained in the control of Westminster but, in a campaign taking place within the devolved arena, the principal focus was on how the rivals for Scottish government would deploy whatever powers they have.

We should not overstate the case. This election was 'more Scottish than British' rather than purely Scottish. A substantial proportion of SES respondents reported choosing in 2011 'mainly according to what was going on in Britain as a whole'. However, even this is unlikely to reflect calculations of Westminster's constitutional pre-eminence. There are two more plausible explanations. The first is simply that, even in a Scottish election, some UK-level considerations will supervene. In 2011 these were often macro-economic but, as we will see in the next chapter, party choice was also influenced by attitudes to the party leaders at Westminster. The two political worlds may be distinct but they still overlap or, at least, they are not closed off from one another. Second, we should not overstate the passivity of voters. Some are simply more interested in one arena than another and are therefore likely to focus on that arena when voting. These individual differences in focus and interest are clearly correlated with partisan preferences: SNP supporters, predictably enough, are disproportionately likely to report voting on Scottish matters, while supporters of Labour and the Conservatives have been less inclined to shift focus to Holyrood following devolution. To that extent, the fact that this election was 'more Scottish than British' in itself helps to explain the SNP's victory.

6
Party Choice in 2011

Those seeking to explain voting behaviour and election outcomes are prone to treat voters as a single actor. Journalists discuss whether the electorate was 'content' or 'hesitant' or 'ready for change', implying some sort of collective mind-set or motivation. Academics have written about *The American Voter* (Campbell et al. 1960) and *Performance Politics and the British Voter* (Clarke et al. 2009), the archetypal singular implying homogeneity in the way that voters make their decisions. These are drastic over-simplifications. Any major election involves thousands (if not millions) of voters as well as hundreds of candidates, dozens of issues, and several parties and leaders. The electorate contains the contented and the discontented, the hesitant and the gung-ho, those keen for change and those preferring the status quo, and so on. Voters also differ in the way that they reach their decisions: some will be guided by performance, others by a long-standing affinity with a particular party, still others choose a preferred leader, and of course many are influenced by a combination of such factors but weighted to different degrees. Yet it is precisely this complexity which means that some simplification is inevitable. Any intelligible explanation of an election outcome requires us to pick out those factors that were most important, and any useful model of party choice can allow only a limited typology of voters and their modes of decision.

Striking a balance between over-simplification and over-complication is an important task for this final chapter. The chapter serves three main purposes. First, we present the results of our full multi-variate models of party choice. This identifies the issues and factors that did most to drive voting behaviour in 2011. We then link these findings to our evidence from elsewhere in the book about how parties were perceived and rated in this election cycle. For instance, it is not enough to know that voters were influenced by their attitudes to the party leaders; leadership can only be an important factor in the election outcome if there were clear disparities in the overall evaluations of these leaders. So our second purpose is to offer an explanation of the 2011 outcome based on combining these two types of survey results: what mattered, and how the parties rated on what mattered. Third, in the concluding section, we broaden the focus to sketch a more general model of party choice in Scottish Parliament elections and to contrast this with Scottish voting behaviour in other contexts, not only Westminster elections but also the upcoming referendum on independence.

Models of party choice in 2011

During the previous four chapters, we have examined a huge range of potential influences on voting behaviour in 2011, and built up a detailed profile of Scottish public opinion at the time of that election. Yet the relevance of these analyses hinges on assumptions that the variables involved did indeed affect party choice in 2011. Many of those assumptions seem highly plausible given previous research, which has shown for example that a perceived commitment to Scottish interests is an important asset for parties contesting Holyrood elections, and that a popular leader is an asset for a party in more or less any electoral setting. Yet they remain assumptions in the context of the 2011 election until, as in this section, we test them more formally.

That testing is achieved by the same technique of multinomial logistic regression that was introduced in Chapter 2 and used there to sketch the socio-demographic profile of each party's electorate. This method allows us to include all of the potential influences on party choice simultaneously and thus to assess whether each exerts an *independent* impact on party choice – that is, whether it improves our prediction of voting behaviour even when all of the other influences are taken into account as well. The premise underlying this approach is that a variable can only contribute to an explanation of the election outcome if it is shown to have such a separate and independent impact. If, for example, voters' evaluations of a party's leader are unrelated to the probability of voting for that party when we also consider attitudes towards that party and its record and policies, then we can reasonably conclude that leadership was not a major influence on that party's performance.

That logic, and this approach in general, represents another compromise between over-simplifying and over-complicating. It is over-simplified because including all of the variables at once neglects the casual interrelations between them. If voters' evaluations of a party's leader in turn influence their perception of that party's competence, then it becomes more difficult to interpret results in which competence has a significant association with party choice but leader evaluations do not. This would not necessarily mean that leadership had no influence; it might simply mean that the effect of leadership was through competence – that is, leaders matter because of how they shape their party's image. Of course, as noted in Chapter 3, the problem is that these causal interrelations are entangled. Take any pair of attitudinal or perceptual variables – attitudes to leaders, perceptions of party image, approval of policies, competence evaluations and so on – and there is good reason to suppose that each might affect the other. Allowing for this would be fiendishly complicated, would require more waves of data collection and many more respondents than we have available here, and even then we would be unable fully to disentangle these causal chains. So including all of these variables at once is a simplification, but a necessary one.

The same issue of causal direction generates another dilemma: that is, whether to include party identification as a predictor variable in these models of party choice. We rehearsed the arguments in Chapter 3. On the one hand, longstanding partisan predispositions influence not only voting behaviour but also voters' perceptions and evaluations, and so failing to control for party allegiances may overstate the effect of the latter on the former. On the other hand, there is growing evidence that party identification is not an 'unmoved mover', and that it is itself influenced by the kinds of variables – leader images, policy preferences, competence evaluations – that are included in our models. And that would make 'controlling for' party identification a misleading notion: we would be controlling for a variable that is in fact one route through which the other variables exert their impact. In the models included here, we exclude party identification for two reasons. First, the sheer number and range of independent variables reduces the risk that, by omitting party identification, we will overstate the effect of any one predictor. If the correlation between leader evaluations and vote is due partly to a genuine leadership effect and partly to the fact that both are driven by prior feelings towards a party, then controlling for a variety of evaluations of that party will help to isolate that independent effect of leadership. Second, a more detailed scrutiny of party choice in 2011 (Johns et al. 2013) showed that the substantive conclusions about voting behaviour, especially about the relative importance of the various factors driving it, were unaffected by whether party identification was omitted or included.

There is no such confusion about causal order when it comes to the socio-demographic variables that formed our first multi-variate model (see Figure 2.1). As noted at the time, variables like age, sex and religion are at the beginning of the causal chain – that is, at the mouth of the 'funnel of causality' (Campbell et al. 1960) – leading to vote choice. In order to gauge their impact, it is neither necessary nor even desirable to control for causally posterior variables like issue positions or leader evaluations. Hence the 'socio-demographics only' model presented in Chapter 2 provides the cleanest measure of the (as it turns out, rather limited) impact of these variables. And, while they are also included as controls in the full models presented in this chapter, we do not report the results in full.

As in Chapters 2 and 3, and for the reasons given there, our model of party choice is a multinomial logistic regression based on the regional list vote. Also as before, the full statistical results are confined to an appendix (see Appendix 2) and more digestible versions are presented here. The sheer size of these models means that it makes sense to present the results in two phases. First, in Table 6.1, we show the full list of variables included and use a simple system (plus or minus) to indicate the direction of the relationships when $p \leq .01$ and use bolded signs when the relationship was statistically significant at $p \leq .05$ in each of the three comparisons (Labour vs. each other major party) that make up the multinomial logit models.[1] Second, focusing on those variables which did have a significant and non-negligible effect, we present a series of charts – one for each major party – showing the relative impact of each predictor and thus identifying those variables that did most to shape the election outcome.

Table 6.1 Variables with statistically significant effects in multinomial logit of list vote

	Con (vs. Lab)	LD (vs. Lab)	SNP (vs. Lab)
Issue positions			
Support community sentences		−	
Oppose free prescriptions	+	+	+
More use of tax-varying powers	+		+
Support prison for knife crime	−	−	−
Support tuition fees			
Oppose spending cuts			
Tax-spend scale (increase)			
Green vs. growth scale (growth)	+		
Constitution scale (independence)			+
Performance evaluations			
Standards of health			
Standards of education			
Living standards			
Standards of law and order			
Conservative UK (2010–)	+		+
Lib Dem UK (2010-)			
Labour UK (–2010)			
SNP Scottish (2007–11)	+		+
Labour Scottish (hypothetical 2007–2011)	−	−	−
Economic evaluations			
Expectations – UK economy			
Expectations – Scottish economy			
Handle cuts – Conservatives	+		
Handle cuts – Labour			−
Handle cuts – Lib Dems		+	
Handle cuts – SNP			
Leader evaluations			
Salmond			+
Gray	−		
Goldie		−	
Scott		+	
Cameron	+		+
Clegg	−		
Miliband	−		−
Brown	−		−
Blair			−

Party image

Overall image – Conservatives	+		
Overall image – Labour		–	
Overall image – Lib Dems		+	
Overall image – SNP			
Scottish interests – Conservatives	+		
Scottish interests – Labour	–	–	–
Scottish interests – Lib Dems		+	
Scottish interests – SNP	+	+	+
Campaign tone – Conservatives	+		
Campaign tone – Labour		–	
Campaign tone – Lib Dems	+	+	
Campaign tone – SNP			

Note: signs indicate direction of relationship, where signs in bold $p \leq .05$, otherwise $p \leq .1$
Sources: SES pre- and post-election surveys.

Table 6.1 is particularly useful in highlighting those variables that turned out to have no independent influence over electoral choice in 2011. Sometimes this has more to do with the parties than with the voters. For example, neither the Likert item on spending cuts ('In the current economic climate, the government should maintain the size of the public sector') nor the 0–10 tax-spending scale (see Figure 4.1) showed a significant association with party choice. This is not because voters do not care or are of one mind when it comes to the public finances; rather, it is because the major parties – especially Labour and the SNP but with the Conservatives only a partial exception – offer little choice on that issue.

Other non-significant variables tell us about how voters simplify the decision making process. Voters' assessments of outcomes in specific issue domains (see Table 4.2) had no separate impact on party choice in 2011. More strikingly, given the context of the election, economic expectations also had no significant effect. Instead, it was the *overall performance evaluations* – of the SNP in office, and Labour had it been in office – that drove voting behaviour. Of course, specific policies, events and economic evaluations will feed into those overall assessments – we are certainly not arguing that the government's record on health, crime or the economy is irrelevant. The point is rather that, when it comes to polling day, it is the overall impression – what Fiorina would call the 'running tally' – that matters rather than the detailed information that built it.

A different type of simplification is shown by the non-significance of the Liberal Democrat performance variable. Rather than trying to assess separately the contributions of the two Westminster coalition partners, voters look to have judged this basically as a Conservative government. On this reading, the Liberal Democrats' very poor showing in the 2011 election is owed to their decision to join the Conservatives in the first place rather than to their perceived performance in that coalition. This is consistent with the party's trajectory in the opinion polls. Another notable feature of the overall performance evaluations is that Labour's record as the outgoing Westminster government looks to have done little to win or lose the party votes in 2011. What mattered was how voters thought that Labour would have performed in office at Holyrood. To that extent, the 2011 Holyrood election was more of a first-order contest; however, the significant effects of Conservative performance at Westminster show that some UK-level considerations continue to bear on voting in Scottish Parliament elections.

One final pair of variables that is noticeably non-significant is the ratings of the SNP's general image and the tone of its campaigning in particular. It seems that the cornerstones of the party's success were the more tangible aspects of 'performance politics', notably the favourable assessments of its record at Holyrood and the popularity of Alex Salmond. This is not to say that the intangibles were unimportant; as we have often noted, voters' impressions of a party with a positive image and agenda may bias their perceptions of its record. However, judging by Table 6.1, insofar as image and campaign tone contributed to the SNP's success, it was because the (typically negative) ratings of the other parties will have cost them votes in 2011. As in previous chapters, in order to illustrate the statistically significant effects we show the effect that they have on the predicted probability of voting for each party. Figure 2.1 and the accompanying discussion provide the blueprint for the presentation in this chapter. So, in the upcoming graphs, each bar represents the extent to which that predictor variable increases or reduces the probability that a voter will have opted for that party rather than one of the others. Our method of presenting the data does change in three ways, however. First, because of the much larger number of variables in these models, we do not present the results for all four parties in the same figure but instead provide a chart for each major party. Second, for the same reason, we do not show the effects of all significant variables but instead apply a criterion of minimum importance: only if a variable shifts the probability of voting for a party by at least 0.01 (i.e. one percentage point) do we illustrate its effect. This is a very accommodating criterion, which errs on the side of showing unimportant results rather than of concealing anything important. Third, Figure 2.1 was based only on dummy (i.e. two-category) variables, and thus showed the impact of being in that category (e.g. male) rather than the comparison category. Here we are dealing with variables in a variety of scale formats and so we show in each case the effect of a full-range change in that variable, for example from zero to ten on the Alex Salmond like-dislike scale, or from 'very bad' to 'very good' on the performance evaluation variables.[2]

Before discussing the charts, it is important to reiterate that these graphs show the influence of each factor over voting behaviour, and not their overall impact on the election outcome. In order to understand whether a factor generally benefited the party in question, we need also to consider the evidence from previous chapters about how the party was rated on that variable. For instance, in Figure 6.1, there is a negative effect of Labour's (hypothetical) performance at Holyrood on the probability of voting SNP. But this does not mean that the SNP lost votes overall because of perceptions of Labour's likely performance. The fact that the bar points leftward simply indicates that, among those who evaluated Labour's likely performance more favourably, the probability of an SNP vote was reduced. But we know from Table 4.1 that assessments of Labour were on balance negative, and so the SNP will have made a net gain on that variable.

Figure 6.1 shows the effects of various predictors on the probability of voting SNP. A first point to note is that voters' issue positions offer little help in predicting SNP voting. This is perhaps predictable given the limited policy distance between the party and its chief rivals. More surprising – not least because here there are major differences between the SNP and its rivals – is the rather weak effect of constitutional preferences. Voters closer to the 'independence' end of the constitutional scale, and happier for the Scottish government to flex its fiscal muscle, were indeed likelier to vote for the SNP but less so than we might – and did – expect. One explanation is that the effects of constitutional preferences remain strong but are channelled through the other variables included in the model. Voters who favour

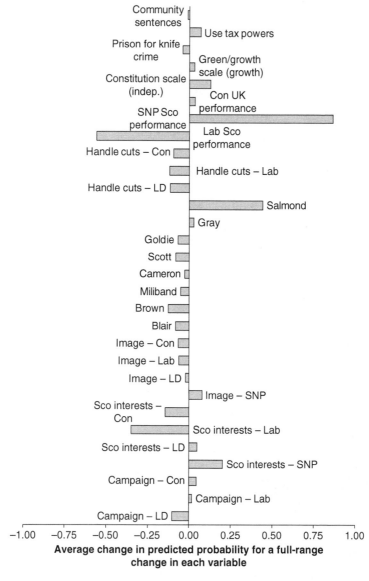

Figure 6.1 Effects of significant variables on the probability of voting SNP
Source: SES pre- and post-election surveys

independence are also prone to like its principal champion, Alex Salmond, and to regard the SNP as particularly committed to Scottish interests, and controlling for these additional variables will tend to dampen the apparent impact of constitutional preferences. There is almost certainly some truth in that explanation. However, it cannot account for why constitutional preferences have become less influential than in the corresponding analyses from the 2007 election (which also included leadership and Scottish interests as mediating variables) (Johns et al. 2009). It does seem that the SNP's appeal has become based less on its flagship constitutional policy; or, more accurately given that voters on the whole reject that policy, we can say that constitutional preferences have become less commonly a reason for voters to reject the party. We return to this point later in the chapter.

If the SNP's appeal is based less on constitutional matters, it is very clear where it lies instead. Comfortably the most influential variable in the entire regression was voters' evaluations of the SNP's performance in office between 2007 and 2011. We remarked in Chapter 4 that these assessments were strikingly favourable and an obvious candidate for explaining the SNP's victory; Figure 6.1 confirms the point. Reinforcing the valence-flavoured nature of the contest between Labour and the SNP, assessments of the former's likely performance were also a powerful influence over support for the latter. Not surprisingly, those who regarded Labour as competent were markedly less likely to vote SNP. The problem for Labour, as noted just above, was that there were not enough such voters.

Attitudes towards Alex Salmond also proved heavily influential over party choice, even controlling for a wide range of partisan preferences. The extent to which the First Minister was an electoral asset should not be overstated because, as Chapter 3 shows, he polarizes opinion rather than winning universal admiration. Nonetheless, the leadership effect in Figure 6.1 combined with his above-average rating means that Alex Salmond was an important plank in the SNP's valence appeal. Both the SNP performance and the Salmond effects were noticeably stronger than in the 2007 election (Johns et al. 2009), while the effect of party image, and notably campaign tone, weakened. This is a clear sign that, while voters in 2007 had to rely on their general impression of the then-untested SNP, voters in 2011 had concrete records – of both the government and its First Minister – to go on.

There remained a specifically Scottish dimension to the SNP's valence appeal, however. Although the party's own rating on handling 'cuts from Westminster' did not prove a significant influence over voting behaviour, it will have gained from the widespread scepticism about the Conservatives and Liberal Democrats in that regard. On the key general indicator of concern for Scottish interests, Figure 6.1 shows that the SNP will have gained both from their own strong rating and from any doubts about Labour's credentials. However, as Table 4.7 confirms, Labour's perceived commitment to Scottish interests was not as widely questioned as their general competence. So the strong effect in Figure 6.1 of Labour's Scottish interests rating will have translated into little overall effect on the SNP. Labour was able to prevent support leaking to the SNP to the extent that it could persuade voters that it was also standing up for Scotland.

That brings us to Figure 6.2 and the factors influencing the probability of voting for Labour. Indeed, these results closely parallel those from Figure 6.1, re-emphasizing that the election was first and foremost a valence battle between the incumbent SNP and its only realistic challenger for office. Position issues are again largely irrelevant, with just small effects for constitutional preferences indicating that Labour has largely become, if anything, a party for those sceptical not just about independence but even about the use of Holyrood's tax powers. Performance was again overwhelmingly important: those (a substantial minority) who thought Labour would have performed well were far more likely to vote for the party; those (a clear majority) who thought the SNP had performed well were far less likely to vote Labour.

Leadership mattered too, but a good deal less and in a way that graphically illustrates the difference in profile between the two contenders for First Minister. The probability of voting for Labour was clearly negatively associated with ratings for Alex Salmond, but was unaffected by voters' attitudes to the party's own leader, Iain Gray. The latter's lacklustre showing may have contributed to doubts about Labour's general performance but overall, rather than costing his party votes as was suggested in much critical campaign coverage, Gray seems instead to have been largely peripheral to the outcome. Perhaps because of Iain Gray's relative obscurity, it was Labour's Westminster leaders who mattered in 2011 and there is at least some

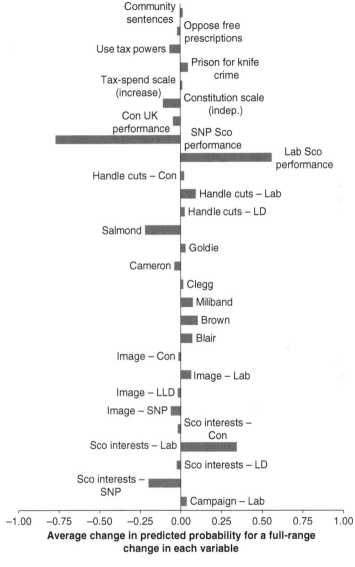

Figure 6.2 Effects of significant variables on the probability of voting Labour

Source: Pre- and post-election surveys

sign of the sympathy vote for Gordon Brown. The less favourable evaluations of Miliband and especially Blair (see Table 3.7) mean that they will, if anything, have cost the party a few votes.

Again in parallel to the SNP analysis, the only other factor that strongly influenced voters' likelihood of choosing Labour was the Scottish interests ratings, and, again, evaluations of both major parties mattered. As noted above, because Labour was almost equally widely trusted and distrusted in terms of commitment to Scottish interests, the net electoral effect of its rating will have been negligible. However, the fact that Labour was much less popular among those crediting the SNP with commitment to Scottish interests, coupled with the fact that the large majority of voters fell into that category, means a considerable loss of support and thus another reason why the party eventually trailed so far behind in second place.

Moving to the Conservative analysis, we first notice the rather smaller size of the graph (Figure 6.3). Not only did fewer of the variables have a noteworthy impact on the probability of voting Conservative in 2011, but none of those impacts were on anything like the scale of the performance effects in the SNP and Labour analyses. In a sense, this reinforces our conclusion about the importance of 'performance politics' in 2011: because the Conservatives were not realistic contenders for office, it is harder to predict why voters would or would not support them. However, this valence account does not extend to second-order voting based on UK-level performance. Voting for the Conservatives in 2011 was almost unaffected by perceptions of the party's record at Westminster; more attention was paid to the Holyrood party's capacity – widely seen as very limited – to manage the impact on Scotland of the coalition's budget cuts. Some voters were also mindful of the Conservatives' broader commitment to defending Scottish interests. In neither the specific nor the general variable case will these effects have worked to the party's advantage (see Table 4.7).

There is also little sign that the Conservatives will have gained from having, in Annabel Goldie, a relatively popular leader. As in the Labour analysis, and reinforcing the dominant position of Alex Salmond, the probability of voting Conservative was more influenced by attitudes to the First Minister than by attitudes to the party's own leader. Also as in the Labour analysis, the party's Scottish leader seems to have been overshadowed by a prominent figure at Westminster.

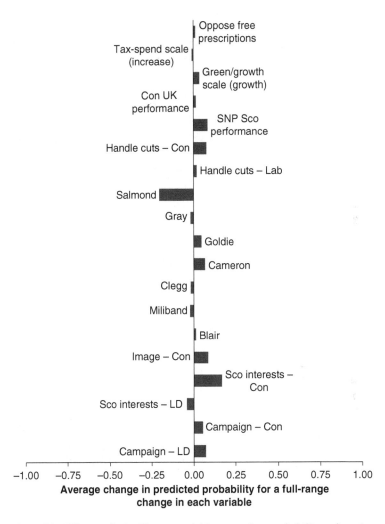

Figure 6.3 Effects of significant variables on the probability of voting Conservative

Source: Pre- and post-election surveys

Table 3.7 confirms that the Conservatives would have been better off had voters focused on Annabel Goldie more than on David Cameron.

A final notable feature of the Conservative results is the very weak effects of issue positions. There are two reasons why this is surprising:

first, at least among the major parties, the Conservatives offer the most distinctive ideological or policy profile; second, as the party was unlikely to achieve office, we would expect its voters to be assessing its policies more than its expected performance. Yet, even though several of the issues that we asked about bear on the left-right scale on which the Conservatives are at least somewhat separated from the other parties, there is virtually no sign of an ideological vote. And there was not even any significant effect of constitutional preferences, despite the party's strongly unionist history. All of this reinforces the impression that the party is confined to a rump of partisans with a fairly distinctive socio-demographic profile but unable to attract new voters to its ideas and programme.

If it proved rather harder to predict voting for the Conservatives than for the two major parties, it proved all but impossible to account for Liberal Democrat support. That is a familiar story from UK elections (Fieldhouse and Russell 2001) but this is an extreme case of that general tendency. Compared to the 45 variables in Table 6.1, Figure 6.4 reports just seven effects, none of them anything more than meagre in size. The few that stand out at all can help to explain the party's poor showing. Liberal Democrat voting was significantly less likely among those that distrusted the party's ability to handle the cuts and those that rated its Scottish leader unfavourably, and both groups were comfortable majorities in the electorate. In such an uneventful graph, it is more instructive to consider the dogs that did not bark and, of these, probably the most obvious are attitudes to Nick Clegg and evaluations of the Liberal Democrats' performance in government at Westminster. It would stretch credulity beyond breaking point to argue that the party's plummeting poll ratings since forming the 2010 coalition had nothing to do with its disastrous showing in 2011, and indeed that it is not what is implied by the (non-) findings in Figure 6.4. We reach here the limits of what the SES can do to explain a shift in opinion that happened almost a year earlier. Our survey can tell us that, in May 2011, those who liked Nick Clegg more were not noticeably more likely to vote Liberal Democrat in the Scottish Parliament election. This is indeed counter-intuitive. However, it is consistent with the idea that the Liberal Democrats, by joining the Conservatives in coalition, had by June 2010 ensured their rejection by the vast majority of Scottish voters. Some of these came to dislike Clegg intensely, others were a little more forgiving,

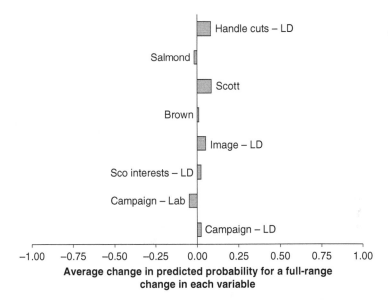

Figure 6.4 Effects of significant variables on the probability of voting Liberal Democrat
Source: Pre- and post-election surveys.

but neither group voted Liberal Democrat anyway and so the impact of evaluations of Clegg on party choice is negligible.

Explaining the outcome

We referred earlier in the chapter to the risk of an over-simplified account of the election. Yet these graphs suggest that a simple account is justified. Party choice in 2011 was driven overwhelmingly by overall assessments of the SNP's record in office and Labour's likely performance had it been in power. As the SNP enjoyed a big lead over Labour on that yardstick, the outcome of the election – and the unanticipated scale of SNP victory – is thus also straightforwardly explained. This election was a clear case of 'performance politics'.

Of course, this simply pushes the question back a causal stage: we then need to explain why it is that the SNP's record was evaluated so much more positively than Labour's expected performance? For this reason, it would be premature to conclude that the other factors discussed in this book – even those which, according to Table 6.1, had no significant effect on party choice – were unimportant. Those factors are quite likely to have fed in to the performance evaluations that then proved so important. For instance, voters who share a party's policy orientation are more likely to be satisfied with its performance, because one aspect of performance is enacting those preferred policies. Yet the broader conclusion about 'performance politics' remains valid. The dominance of performance evaluations in the regression results suggests that most of the other variables matter largely – in some cases only – insofar as they shape evaluations or expectations of performance. And this is a noteworthy conclusion in the broader context of electoral research because such variables have generally been regarded as having an independent impact. The argument was not that voters support the party closest to them ideologically merely because they would then expect that party to perform best in office; proximity was held to be desirable for other reasons. This would lead us to expect an association between policy positions and party choice even when controlling for performance evaluations and, indeed, such an effect does show up in parallel models of voting at UK general elections (e.g. Clarke et al. 2009, 2011). Proximity matters in general elections, then, even if 'performance politics' still prevails. It is in this Scottish Parliament election that the valence model dominates the proximity model so completely.

This might be thought counter-intuitive given that it is the majoritarian electoral system at Westminster that is held to encourage policy convergence and thus encourage valence voting, while proportional systems allow for more ideological diversity. However, we need to consider the party system as well as the electoral system and, in particular, the absence of the Conservatives as serious contenders in Scotland. This means that the leading rivals for office at Westminster, even if they have converged dramatically in comparison with the polarized 1980s, remain more distinct than the leading rivals at Holyrood. Aside from the constitutional issue, voters find virtually no difference between Labour and the SNP. In this context, electoral competition based largely on performance is exactly what we would expect (Green 2007).

Before continuing, we should address a reason why some might be sceptical about the powerful performance effects observed in our analyses. The problem, known technically as 'endogeneity', is that performance evaluations might be thought the *consequence* rather than the *cause* of voting intentions. The argument runs thus: those who already intend to vote for a party for other reasons will tend to evaluate its record more favourably, and to decry those of its rivals, and so we would see a strong correlation between performance assessments and party choice without any implication that the former drive the latter. This complaint is particularly compelling where performance evaluations are collected in a post-election survey, when the vote has already been cast. However, it also carries force in situations like this one where vote is predicted by pre-election evaluations, because many people will already have made up their mind by then and so already have the incentive to bring their performance evaluations into line with their vote intention. Yet there are four reasons to believe that our conclusion about performance politics stands firm.

The first is that these very detailed models of party choice include controls for most of the 'other reasons' that could drive vote intention. Many voters will indeed have already decided to vote for the SNP because of its constitutional stance, its commitment to Scottish interests, its leader, and so on, but these variables cannot explain the performance effects because they are held constant in the regression analyses. Second, the evaluations of SNP performance were retrospective. Expectations of future records are more uncertain, more impressionistic and thus more likely to be contaminated by partisan bias. By contrast, as we saw in Chapter 4, there was a fair degree of consensus about the SNP's showing – much more so than we would expect if evaluations simply reflected party sympathies. A third reason is that we would expect endogeneity bias to afflict any explicitly partisan variable in the model. Those who already like a party should give favourable ratings not only to its performance but also to its image, campaigning, ability to handle spending cuts, and so on. Why, then, was it the performance variables that had the strongest associations with party choice? The obvious answer is that they are indeed the most important influence on voting behaviour. Fourth, by considering only those who were not sure how they would vote at the time of the pre-election survey, we can isolate a group whose performance evaluations are less likely to be biased by partisan predispositions. In an analysis of those 'undecided' voters, the performance effects were just as strong as in – indeed, slightly stronger than – the sample as a whole. Again, the explanation most consistent with the empirical evidence is that performance assessments really did drive the eventual party choice.

However, performance evaluations were not the only thing that mattered. Leadership was, in some form or other, a significant and often quite a powerful predictor of support for all four parties. Attitudes to Alex Salmond were clearly and strongly influential over the propensity to vote for the SNP, Labour and the Conservatives (see Figures 6.1–6.3). No other leader left anything like that stamp on the election and, indeed, accusations that Iain Gray was an insignificant figure are borne out by the fact that evaluations of the Scottish Labour leader had no statistically significant effect. Nonetheless, overall, leader evaluations were second only to performance evaluations in the Labour and SNP analyses and were the strongest (if, in absolute terms, still rather weak) effects on choice for the other two parties.

In referring to leadership as having an effect distinct from – that is, over and above – that of performance, we diverge from the interpretation of leader effects put forward by Clarke et al. (2004, 2009, 2011) in their analyses of UK general election voting. They regard leaders principally as a heuristic device to judge parties' likely performance. If voters see a competent leader, they anticipate competent performance from his or her party. This may well be the case but, as assessments of party performance are extensively controlled in our regression analyses, there is obviously more to leadership voting than a competence heuristic. Leaders might also be a cue to party characteristics other than competence. Stevens et al. (2011) find that, in the 2010 general election, trustworthiness was the leadership trait that did most to influence voting behaviour, and voters might reasonably infer that the party of a trustworthy leader is more likely to keep its promises. Yet we also control for that latter variable as part of the party image variable. Indeed, insofar as the key characteristics of parties are held constant in analyses like these, any remaining leader effects look like a more direct or 'pure' effect of leadership. Voters are simply more likely to vote for a party whose leader's personality appeals to them, an effect greatly magnified when that personality is as prominent and familiar as that of Alex Salmond.

This point is reinforced by the effects of evaluations of Westminster figures. If leadership was simply a cue to party competence, then these figures would be irrelevant because they were not up for election and cannot – except highly indirectly – influence the performance of the Scottish government. (Some of them were retired, in any case.) However, setting aside the dominant figure of Salmond, the evaluations of various Westminster leaders proved, if anything, more influential than those of Iain Gray, Annabel Goldie and Tavish Scott. That is consistent with a simple 'personality voting' account of leadership effects. Together, prominence and popularity (or unpopularity) are sufficient conditions for a leader to win (or lose) his or her party votes.

To recap: the single most important reason for the outcome of the 2011 election was the strongly positive assessment of the SNP's term in office. A second plank in the party's victory was the popularity of Alex Salmond, who was not only rated a good deal more favourably than any of his Holyrood contenders but was also quite a lot more popular than he had been in 2007, which helps to explain why the SNP was able to extend its margin of victory so dramatically. (Iain Gray's rating was no better than Jack McConnell's unimpressive evaluations in 2007, thus also helping to explain why Labour's vote share remained steady.)

The third important factor is the SNP's clear advantage over Labour – and massive advantage over the other parties – in terms of 'looking after Scottish interests'. Like leadership, this variable was important across the regressions: that is, the prospects of all four parties depended at least to some extent on whether they were seen as defending Scotland. When it comes to the central battle between the SNP and Labour, there was an interesting asymmetry on the 'Scottish interests' effects – it was perceptions of Labour that mattered more. The likeliest reason for this is that Labour's credentials were more in doubt. As Table 4.7 confirms, most voters credited the SNP with a strong commitment to Scottish interests, regardless of whether they supported the party. Put another way, there was little scope for the 'Scottish interests' variable to discriminate between those who did and those who did not vote for the SNP. (A parallel argument can be made about the more specific issue of managing the impact of spending cuts from Westminster. Voters' generally positive endorsements of the SNP on this criterion turned out to matter little; it was evaluations of Labour that mattered more. Because, as Table 4.7 also shows, Labour had a more mixed report, this 'defending Scotland against the cuts' variable was not the vote-winner that the party's strategists appear to have thought it would be.)

When respondents judge whether a party 'looks after' or 'defends' Scottish interests, an obvious question is: against what? One of the limitations of such survey data is that we lack detailed information in answer to that question. However, the accumulated evidence points to some conclusions. First, this is not some kind of extension of the constitutional issue. Certainly there should be no implication that those who opposed devolution in the first place, or who oppose 'more powers' or independence now, are any less keen to defend Scottish interests. Instead, it probably has more to do with fighting Scotland's corner within whatever are the current constitutional arrangements. But even that may be too narrow an interpretation of what is potentially a very broad notion. There may well be widespread disagreement about what it means to serve Scottish interests, as well as about how they would be best served. Where there is no significant disagreement is in *whether* they should be served. That is why, in previous discussions, we have referred to Scottish interests as a valence issue (Johns et al. 2010, 2013). Voters might vary in the extent to which they feel British as well as Scottish, and disagree about the constitutional arrangements that best serve Scotland, but they are more or less unanimous in wanting the Scottish government to deliver the best deal for the country. Put another way, this is the Scottish dimension of 'performance politics'. In a Scottish Parliament election, impressions of a party's willingness and ability to defend Scottish interests are an important component of overall performance evaluations.

The SNP has long been highly regarded in this respect. 'Standing up for Scotland's interests' is one of the two core goals enshrined in the party's constitution and is a point that seems to be acknowledged even by those who do not support its other goal of independence. The SNP's favourable ratings on 'Scottish interests' recorded in Table 4.7 are an echo of Miller's (1981) finding that the party's 1970s breakthrough was widely regarded, even by Labour and Conservative sympathizers, as a good thing for Scotland. The other main parties' reputations in terms of defending Scottish interests are, at best, much less secure. One obvious reason for this is that, while the formal structures and relationships may vary, all three are in some sense Scottish versions of a British party. As such, the credentials of the Scottish party depend in part on events and policies at Westminster. In the 1980s and 1990s, Labour won considerable credit for defending Scottish interests, being a left-leaning (and the only realistic) opposition to a Conservative government seen as anti-Scottish. The downturn in Labour's reputation in this regard followed their return to power at Westminster, and Table 4.7 confirms that the Conservatives and Liberal Democrats also lost ground on 'Scottish interests' on taking power at the UK level.

In this context, and with a view to explaining the 2011 outcome, the most pertinent question is why Labour saw only a negligible improvement in its reputation for defending Scotland following its 2010 defeat at Westminster. The party certainly seemed to anticipate more of a boost, judging by its main 2011 campaign strategy which, at least until the final days before polling, was to try to reawaken Scottish hostility towards the Conservatives. Such hostility probably was reawakened – indeed, it had not exactly been dormant anyway – but there are two reasons why Labour was not a beneficiary. First, devolution made the SNP into a credible contender for government in Scotland and thus a rival to Labour when it comes to defending Scottish interests against the perceived threat posed by a Conservative government at Westminster. Second, as we showed in Chapter 4, Labour's commitment to Scottish interests has been somewhat undermined by its constitutional stance, notably the perceived opposition to further devolution (see also Johns et al. 2010, ch. 5). By contrast, the SNP's commitment to independence wins it credit for fighting for Scottish interests, even among opponents of these constitutional options. The upshot is that the SNP currently looks the more credible repository of anti-Tory feeling and so, following the Conservatives' return to power at Westminster, it was the SNP's rather than Labour's Scottish interests rating that increased significantly.

How Scotland votes today

Conspicuously absent from that account of the 2011 election outcome was the constitutional issue that has been central to Scottish political debate, and to the winning party's platform, for decades. One reason for this is precisely because the issue is so familiar. Many voters have very firmly held nationalist or unionist views, and these long-held constitutional preferences will often have cemented into enduring identifications with the parties that share them. The result is that the votes of those who strongly oppose or strongly support independence are largely determined long before polling day. In turn, the constitutional issue is less useful in explaining electoral change and hence election outcomes. Certainly the constitution cannot explain the sharp increase in SNP support between 2007 and 2011 – just as it could not explain the party's similarly major gains between 2003 and 2007 – because, as any observer of Scottish public opinion knows, support for independence has basically flatlined during that entire period. The period since devolution has seen considerable electoral volatility but very little change in constitutional preferences, reinforcing the point that the latter is not driving the former. Put bluntly, we know that this election was won on performance because the SNP could not and would not have won it on policy.

There is a distinction between explaining an overall election outcome and explaining individual voters' decisions. The constitutional issue is more useful for the latter purpose: there remain significant numbers of voters who will invariably vote for or against the SNP because of its pro-independence stance. It was the only position issue that showed much sign of electoral importance, unsurprisingly given that it is the only such issue on which the leading contenders take – and are perceived as taking – sharply differing positions. However, we noted in discussing Figure 6.1 that the constitution seems to be diminishing in its influence over party choice. One reason for this in 2011 was that the economy took centre stage, reducing the proportion of voters citing any other major issue – including independence – as the most important in their voting decision. Yet it was not the economic variables that drove party choice in 2011. The importance of the constitutional issue has instead waned relative to that of more general valence variables like performance, leadership and Scottish interests. And it is implausible to argue, along the lines sketched earlier, that the latter variables are simply the channel through which constitutional preferences take electoral effect. Of course, those who favour independence are more likely to evaluate the SNP and Alex Salmond more favourably. But there are too few supporters of independence to generate the kind of positive evaluations of the SNP's record, image and leadership that were recorded in the 2011 SES. What has happened over the past two elections, then, is that the SNP built up an election-winning coalition of support, of which longstanding supporters of independence form the foundation but represent a dwindling proportion. The newer 'recruits' to the party are attracted by the key variables in our 'performance politics' model, and those have now become the most potent predictors of an SNP vote. There is a parallel here with evidence from a late 2007 survey of the SNP membership. It showed that those who joined the party more recently – notably in the surge following reorganization and Salmond's resumption of the leadership in 2004 – were markedly less likely to cite independence as their main reason for signing up, and more likely instead to mention the party's leadership, its commitment to Scottish interests, or some other more performance-related endorsement of the party (Mitchell et al. 2011). Given the evidence presented in this book, and the fact that the SNP's membership has grown quickly alongside its vote share, we might reasonably expect that trend to have continued, even accelerated. Again, then, the relative importance of support for independence within the SNP can be seen as having declined.

Turning back to electoral support, we might interpret the strongly valence-flavoured basis of the SNP's 2011 vote as showing the success of the party's strategic approach. Summarized crudely, this was to emphasize its governing competence and, as far as possible, to allay fears about independence. As the SNP vote increases (but support for independence does not), it follows that the proportion of SNP voters who support its flagship policy is declining. The party therefore has an incentive to downplay its constitutional ambitions or, at least, to emphasize its other offerings. Its commitment to a referendum was the foundation stone of this strategy in 2011 as in 2007. Besides, of course, voters in 2011 could look back on a term of SNP government – albeit, crucially, a minority administration – during which the prospect of independence had apparently advanced no further. As we saw in Chapter 4, all of this served to weaken in voters' minds any association between an SNP victory and the likelihood of Scottish independence. And, again as in 2007, the party was thus able to maximize the electoral profit accruing from its advantages on key valence criteria.

Now that the SNP has won a majority and was thus able to legislate for an independence referendum in October 2014, any strategy of downplaying the party's commitment to independence has obviously to be shelved. More generally, the relationship between

Holyrood election outcomes and Scotland's constitutional future is set to change. Given the uncertainty over the referendum result, it is difficult and probably fruitless to speculate on the nature of that change. What we can argue with more confidence is that 'performance politics' looks likely to remain a convincing explanation for Scottish Parliament election outcomes. One reason for this is that there seems no immediate prospect of ideological divergence. While the leading parties retain broadly similar outlooks and objectives, voters have little option but to choose according to which contender seems most likely to achieve these shared aims.

But there are less contingent reasons, too. First, while it would be an exaggeration to talk of two-party politics, a party system has emerged wherein the two leading contenders are large enough to be the only plausible contenders to lead a government. Second, there is the arrival of 'alternance': that is, the alternating of those two major parties in power. As we noted in Chapter 4, most Scottish voters by 2011 had had experience of both Labour and the SNP in office, and that encourages valence comparisons between the two. In 2007, the SNP was for many a potentially attractive option but the party was largely untested in office (even at local government level). And a likely contributing factor in the party's positive evaluations in 2011 is a sense of reassurance, even relief, that this novice party of government had not only averted disaster but enjoyed a relatively tranquil term.

It is not only the party system that is bedding in following devolution. The Scottish Parliament is using more of the powers available to it; and, in turn, citizens come to recognize its role and impact on their lives. Voters are slowly but steadily perceiving more at stake in Scottish elections and the more that the elected government can do, the more its performance matters. Second-order elections give voters the freedom to express their preferences, often for smaller and radical parties; in first-order contests, which Scottish elections increasingly resemble, there is more incentive for valence voting. If the Scottish government were seen as economically impotent, an election in the context of 2011 would have been a highly second-order affair with voters preoccupied by – and commenting on – the attempts of the Westminster government to address the ongoing crisis. In fact, however, voters credited the Scottish government with considerable influence over economic outcomes, and those who reported this as their 'most important issue' when voting were as likely to have the Scottish economy as the British economy in mind. The SNP was thus able to profit from its favourable rating in terms of handling the Scottish economy; and Labour gained less than it might have hoped from its advantage when it came to dealing with economic problems at the UK level.

This dual focus of economic voting in 2011 is one example of a broader consequence of devolution. Scottish politics and elections are increasingly a distinct sphere – and not one that simply orbits around Westminster. There are new political institutions with significant powers, distinctively Scottish issues and public policies, a strikingly different party system, and so on, all of this covered by Scottish media increasingly focused on these new 'domestic' politics. In this context, it makes more sense to talk about Scottish and UK politics in terms of parallel arenas rather than multiple levels. Hierarchy is inherent in the notion of first- and second-order elections, with choice at any given election driven by the level identified as more important or powerful. However, as noted in Chapter 5, there is reason to suppose that *absolute* importance matters more than *relative* importance. We would expect Scottish Parliament elections to be predominantly Scottish affairs, not because they have supplanted Westminster elections as first order, but because they are now the recognized 'general' elections in an arena regarded by voters, parties and the media as important.

Again, there is a danger of over-simplifying here. There remains a significant minority of voters that is focused on British politics even at Scottish elections. This is not merely a historical legacy of the pre-devolution era; it is encouraged by the fact that three of the main four parties in Scottish elections are the three main players at Westminster. As the case of the Liberal Democrats in 2011 shows, it is unrealistic to expect voters carefully to distinguish between the policies, records and images of the British and Scottish versions of the same party. So we would expect events and personalities from the Westminster arena to influence voting in Scottish Parliament elections – and vice versa. Nonetheless, the evidence is clear that Scottish Parliament elections are increasingly determined by Scottish-level factors. Figures 6.1–6.4 made the point very clearly by illustrating both the supreme importance of SNP and Labour performance at Holyrood and the negligible influence carried by evaluations of the governing parties at Westminster.

This notion of distinct political arenas, each with its own general election, can explain the drastically different outcomes of the 2010 general election in Scotland and the 2011 Scottish Parliament election. There is no great puzzle in the fact that Labour performed far better in the first than the second while the SNP did the opposite, and no implication that either election is therefore anything other than first order. Quite simply, Labour was the only plausible challenger to the Conservatives in 2010, a popularity contest that it won with ease, and the only plausible challenger to the SNP in 2011, a popularity contest that it lost by a similar margin. Just as the 2010 election turned out to have minimal implications for the 2011 results, this Scottish Parliament election tells us little about how Scotland will vote in the next UK general election in 2015. That contest is too far away for it to be worth further speculation here; what we can say, however, is that the outcome will be determined by factors belonging in that same Westminster arena.

Further strong support for the idea of parallel political arenas comes from our multi-level party identification experiment, which tended to replicate the results of the 2010 and 2011 elections depending on whether respondents were primed to consider Westminster or Holyrood politics respectively. It is quite common for voters to have two distinct and potentially conflicting party allegiances, one applying in the Scottish and one in the British political arena. Indeed, the word 'conflicting' may mislead here because, given the different electoral and party systems and hence the different incentives facing voters in the different arenas, they may pursue exactly the same goals by supporting a different party depending on the arena in question. For example, the most common 'mixed' identification was to support Labour at the UK level but the SNP at the Scottish level. Many voters may regard this as the most viable combination for defending Scottish interests in the two arenas. In any case, it is clear that voters not only distinguish two political arenas but form distinct attitudes and preferences accordingly.

Two of our conclusions are worth reiterating here. First, the 2011 Scottish Parliament election took place in its own sphere, distinct from and certainly not eclipsed by that of Westminster politics.

Second, the constitutional question was neither a pivotal factor nor even among the most important determinants of party choice. This election was a particularly vivid illustration of the general rule that voters distinguish between choosing a Scottish government and choosing a constitutional future. Together, those conclusions make clear that the 2011 results give little or no guidance about the outcome of the referendum on independence scheduled for October 2014. As with Westminster elections, however, our arguments enable us to say something about the *basis* for voting in the referendum. And here we return to the notion of 'performance politics'. While a large number, perhaps already a majority, of Scottish voters have already made up their minds about independence, that still leaves plenty – enough to swing the outcome either way – who are as yet unresolved. Their decisions are likely to be swayed by practice rather than principle; that is, by whether they think that Scotland will perform better or worse, and be more or less able to defend its own interests, if independent. In that sense, winning this referendum is another test – and the stiffest yet – of the performance politics credentials that won the SNP its surprise majority in 2011.

Appendix 1: The 2011 Scottish Election Study

The 2011 Scottish Election Study (SES) is an ongoing effort to chronicle the Scottish electorate's opinions before and after the Scottish Parliament elections. In addition to the standard pre- and post-election waves (as were conducted in previous Scottish Election Studies), the 2011 study contained a unique panel component, re-interviewing respondents who participated in the 2007 SES. The 2011 study was funded by a grant from the Economic and Social Research Council (ESRC) (ref. 000-22-4539), directed by the authors of this volume and was based in the School of Government and Public Policy at the University of Strathclyde. The data and questionnaires are available on the project's website (www.scottishelectionstudy.org.uk) and have also been archived with the UK Data Archive (www.data-archive.ac.uk).

Data collection

The methodology of the 2011 SES largely reflects that adopted for the 2007 SES. The surveys were conducted over the internet, with the fieldwork being contracted to YouGov, one of the leading internet survey polling firms in the UK. The sample was drawn from YouGov's panel of respondents and was selected to be demographically representative of the Scottish electorate (details on YouGov's fieldwork and methods can be found at www.yougov.co.uk/corporate/about). The study was designed as a two-wave panel, interviewing the same respondents before and after the election. Owing to unforeseen delays, the pre-election survey was not in the field until a week before the election, thus the 2011 SES is limited in what information it can provide about what is usually called the 'long campaign.'

Despite the limitation in covering public opinion over the course of the long campaign, the SES 2011 does have a distinct advantage over similar election surveys. The 2011 SES was able to leverage the fact that YouGov conducted both the 2007 and 2011 surveys to create a panel design between the two election studies. That is, the 2011 survey was able to return to respondents from the 2007 study who were still in the YouGov respondent pool, allowing us to associate the same respondent's answers to the 2007 questionnaire with their 2011 responses. As is detailed in Chapter 5, we are able to leverage this panel design to associate constitutional preferences and party support over the two election cycles. Table A1.1 summarizes the key information on the pre- and post-election waves as well as the 2007–2011 panel.

The SES questionnaires developed by the research team sought to retain continuity over time and further develop the SES time series by incorporating

Wave	Fieldwork dates	N	Response/retention rate (denominator)
1, pre-election	28 April–4 May 2011	2046	61% (sampled respondents)
2, post-election	7–16 May 2011	1763	86% (pre-election respondents)
2007–2011 Panel		767	49% (2007 post-election respondents)

Note: The Scottish Parliament election was held on 5 May 2011.

as much of the question wording from the 2007 SES as the 2011 aims and objectives allowed. The core battery of 'standard' survey questions, measuring relevant predispositions were included in the 2011 survey. In addition to the core battery, new questions were developed to further probe respondent constitutional preferences and responsibility attributions (reflecting the 2011 focus on the multi-level nature of the Scottish elections). Additionally, the 2011 SES included several 'split-half' survey experiments designed to explore multi-level party identification and understanding of political processes

Representativeness and weighting

To adjust for non-response bias, we made use of weighting variables when conducting our analyses. As a general rule, we relied on the weight variables supplied by YouGov, which adjust the observed data to reflect the target sample. The YouGov weight variables take into account respondent demographic and attitudinal variables, including respondent age, gender, social class, region, newspaper readership and past vote. In additional analyses, where appropriate and as indicated in the text, we also employ turnout weights, ensuring that the analysis results match with the actual party choice.

Appendix 2: Full Results of Statistical (Regression) Analyses

This Appendix contains the full results of the various statistical analyses associated with the results presented in graphical form throughout the book. In general, we aimed to make our presentation of statistical results within the chapters as easy to interpret as possible. That said, the more statistically inclined will want to peruse the complete results in the following tables. Here we display the full results of the ordinary least squared regressions, the multinomial logistic regressions and the structural equations model with unstandardized coefficients (except for the structural model which also displays the standardized coefficients). Each table is numbered according to the chapter associated with that analysis, and each table's title indicates the corresponding figure from the main text.

Table A2 2.1 Multinomial logit of regional party choice on demographic characteristics (for Figure 2.1)

	Conservative (vs. Labour)			Lib Dems (vs. Labour)			SNP (vs. Labour)		
	B	s.e.	p =	B	s.e.	p =	B	s.e.	p =
Age 18–34	−0.48	0.36	0.18	0.56	0.47	0.23	−0.07	0.23	0.77
Age 55–81	0.60	0.26	0.02	0.29	0.35	0.41	−0.03	0.18	0.86
Men	0.20	0.22	0.38	−0.20	0.29	0.48	0.18	0.16	0.26
Social class A, B	−0.34	0.30	0.26	−0.70	0.41	0.09	−0.02	0.24	0.94
Social class C2, D, E	−0.75	0.27	0.01	−0.49	0.33	0.14	0.06	0.19	0.74
Education, Vocational	0.86	0.50	0.08	−0.32	1.12	0.78	−0.12	0.35	0.74
Education, Standard grade	0.24	0.38	0.54	0.30	0.53	0.57	−0.31	0.25	0.22
Education, Highers	0.53	0.34	0.12	0.10	0.49	0.85	−0.09	0.22	0.69
Education, Degree	0.90	0.39	0.02	1.10	0.49	0.02	0.21	0.25	0.41
Religion, Catholic	−0.31	0.40	0.44	−1.18	0.94	0.21	−0.39	0.26	0.13
Religion, Church of Scotland	0.39	0.27	0.16	0.52	0.34	0.12	−0.09	0.20	0.66
Religion, Other Protestant	0.95	0.39	0.02	−0.01	0.52	0.98	−0.55	0.31	0.07
Religion, Others	0.10	0.51	0.85	0.40	0.54	0.45	0.01	0.39	0.99
Tabloid readers	0.10	0.35	0.77	−1.00	0.43	0.02	−0.03	0.22	0.88
Broadsheet readers	0.43	0.35	0.22	−0.09	0.39	0.82	0.22	0.23	0.36
Urban resident	−0.29	0.22	0.19	−0.65	0.33	0.05	−0.27	0.16	0.09
Employed in private sector	0.41	0.22	0.07	0.12	0.34	0.72	0.35	0.16	0.03
Trade union member	−0.84	0.22	0.00	−0.63	0.35	0.07	−0.05	0.16	0.77
Constant	−1.40	0.50	0.01	−0.94	0.62	0.13	0.38	0.34	0.28

$N = 1211$ Pseudo $R^2 = .06$

Coefficients in bold $p \leq .05$

Table A2 3.1 OLS regressions of party like/dislike (0–10 scale) on party image assessments, controlling for party identification (for Figure 3.1)

	Conservative like			Labour like			Lib dem like			SNP Like		
	B	s.e.	p =	B	s.e.	p =	B	s.e.	p =	B	s.e.	p =
Image: Capable strong government	1.08	0.14	0.00	1.91	0.15	0.00	1.26	0.23	0.00	2.47	0.17	0.00
Image: United (or divided)	0.64	0.13	0.00	0.87	0.15	0.00	0.55	0.21	0.01	0.44	0.18	0.02
Image: Standing up for Scotland	1.53	0.23	0.00	1.16	0.15	0.00	1.96	0.17	0.00	1.20	0.16	0.00
Image: In touch w/ordinary people	1.15	0.18	0.00	0.92	0.15	0.00	0.68	0.25	0.00	1.49	0.13	0.00
Image: Keep promises	1.70	0.20	0.00	0.83	0.15	0.00	1.32	0.17	0.00	1.15	0.26	0.00
PID: Conservative	2.46	0.25	0.00	-1.16	0.20	0.00	0.42	0.23	0.06	-0.87	0.19	0.00
PID: Labour	-1.08	0.15	0.00	2.10	0.15	0.00	-0.50	0.14	0.00	-0.49	0.14	0.00
PID: Lib Dem	0.36	0.31	0.25	-0.14	0.29	0.64	2.07	0.34	0.00	-0.95	0.29	0.00
PID: SNP	-0.50	0.15	0.00	-0.08	0.14	0.57	-0.28	0.15	0.06	1.88	0.13	0.00
PID: Other	-0.33	0.45	0.47	0.36	0.52	0.49	-0.67	0.48	0.17	-0.19	0.42	0.66
Constant	2.26	0.11	0.00	2.57	0.11	0.00	2.87	0.10	0.00	2.06	0.25	0.00
N	1235			1241			1158			1361		
R2 adj	0.63			0.73			0.51			0.67		

Table A2 3.2 Multinomial logit of regional party choice on leader evaluations and demographic characteristics (for Figure 3.2)

	Conservative (vs. Labour)			Lib Dems (vs. Labour)			SNP (vs. Labour)		
	B	s.e.	p =	B	s.e.	p =	B	s.e.	p =
Age 18–34	−0.55	0.67	0.41	−0.51	0.70	0.47	0.89	0.48	0.07
Age 55–81	−0.75	0.51	0.14	−0.08	0.59	0.90	−0.57	0.40	0.16
Men	0.72	0.46	0.12	−0.59	0.50	0.23	−0.42	0.34	0.21
Social class A,B	0.26	0.53	0.62	−0.25	0.61	0.68	−0.24	0.43	0.57
Social class C1	0.15	0.54	0.78	0.22	0.58	0.71	−0.88	0.40	0.03
Education, Vocational	0.94	1.07	0.38	−1.70	1.68	0.31	−0.41	0.75	0.59
Education, Standard grade	0.64	0.77	0.41	0.64	0.79	0.42	−0.06	0.54	0.91
Education, Highers	0.44	0.63	0.49	0.01	0.74	0.99	0.16	0.48	0.74
Education, Degree	0.56	0.70	0.42	0.85	0.77	0.27	0.08	0.55	0.88
Religion, Catholic	−1.98	0.93	0.03	−2.09	1.51	0.17	0.13	0.52	0.81
Religion, Church of Scotland	−0.57	0.53	0.29	0.65	0.56	0.25	−0.16	0.41	0.70
Religion, Other Protestant	0.40	0.70	0.57	0.00	0.90	1.00	0.16	0.57	0.78
Religion, Others	−0.40	0.80	0.62	0.31	0.87	0.72	−1.80	0.77	0.02
Tabloid readers	−0.94	0.67	0.16	−1.54	0.66	0.02	−1.06	0.47	0.03
Broadsheet readers	−0.28	0.69	0.68	−0.97	0.70	0.16	−0.76	0.52	0.15
Urban resident	−0.11	0.45	0.81	−0.26	0.51	0.61	−0.08	0.34	0.82
Employed in private sector	−0.32	0.45	0.47	0.04	0.52	0.94	−0.10	0.34	0.98
Trade union member	−0.04	0.47	0.94	0.21	0.53	0.69	0.74	0.35	0.04

Table A2 3.2 (Continued)

	Conservative (vs. Labour)			Lib Dems (vs. Labour)			SNP (vs. Labour)		
	B	s.e.	p =	B	s.e.	p =	B	s.e.	p =
PID: Conservative	1.13	0.81	0.16	-2.46	1.35	0.07	-1.31	0.90	0.14
PID: Labour	**-2.14**	**0.87**	**0.01**	**-1.47**	**0.72**	**0.04**	**-1.37**	**0.39**	**0.00**
PID: Lib Dem	-1.87	1.52	0.22	1.73	0.93	0.06	0.12	0.94	0.90
PID: SNP	2.54	1.40	0.07	1.53	1.58	0.33	**3.67**	**1.25**	**0.00**
Alex Salmond (SNP)	0.11	0.08	0.18	0.03	0.09	0.77	**0.81**	**0.08**	**0.00**
Iain Gray (Labour)	**-0.45**	**0.12**	**0.00**	**-0.53**	**0.13**	**0.00**	**-0.36**	**0.08**	**0.00**
Annabel Goldie (Conserv)	**0.37**	**0.11**	**0.00**	**-0.34**	**0.13**	**0.01**	0.02	0.08	0.84
Tavish Scott (Lib Dem)	-0.15	0.13	0.22	**0.69**	**0.17**	**0.00**	-0.18	0.09	0.06
David Cameron (UK Conserv PM)	**0.51**	**0.12**	**0.00**	0.23	0.14	0.11	0.14	0.09	0.12
Nick Clegg (UK Lib Dem)	0.05	0.12	0.69	**0.30**	**0.14**	**0.03**	**0.22**	**0.09**	**0.02**
Ed Miliband (UK Labour)	-0.21	0.12	0.08	-0.25	0.13	0.06	**-0.25**	**0.09**	**0.01**
Gordon Brown (UK Labour PM)	-0.09	0.10	0.40	-0.11	0.12	0.36	-0.07	0.08	0.35
Tony Blair (UK Labour PM)	**-0.24**	**0.09**	**0.01**	-0.05	0.11	0.66	**-0.28**	**0.07**	**0.00**
Constant	-0.12	1.33	0.93	0.48	1.33	0.72	1.26	1.00	0.20

N = 1007 Pseudo R2 = .72
Coefficients in bold *p* ≤ .05

165

Table A2 4.1 Structural model estimates (for Figure 4.2)

Predictors	Dependents	B	s.e.	β
Education scale (exogenous)	SNP like 2007	-0.15	0.03	-0.07
Age (exogenous)	SNP like 2007	0.03	0.00	0.14
National identity (exogenous)	SNP like 2007	-0.86	0.04	-0.38
National identity (exogenous)	Constitutional preference 2007	-0.43	0.04	-0.49
Sex: Men (exogenous)	Constitutional preference 2007	0.17	0.06	0.08
SNP like 2007	Constitutional preference 2007	-0.01	0.02	-0.03
SNP like 2007	SNP competent 2011	0.14	0.02	0.36
SNP like 2007	SNP like 2011	0.43	0.04	0.39
Constitutional preference 2007	SNP like 2007	1.79	0.04	0.69
Constitutional preference 2007	SNP competent 2011	0.15	0.06	0.15
Constitutional preference 2007	Constitutional preference 2011	0.55	0.05	0.51
SNP competent 2011	SNP like 2011	1.68	0.06	0.58
SNP competent 2011	Constitutional preference 2011	0.10	0.07	0.09
SNP like 2011	Constitutional preference 2011	0.07	0.03	0.18
Constitutional preference 2011	SNP like 2011	0.03	0.15	0.01

R² for Dependent variables

Dependents

	R2
SNP like 2007	0.88
Constitutional preference 2007	0.19
SNP competent 2011	0.25
SNP like 2011	0.72
Constitutional preference 2011	0.49

N = 559

Coefficients in bold p ≤ .05

Table A2 6.1 Multinomial logit of regional party choice on attitudinal and demographic predictors (for Figure 6.1)

	Conservative (vs. Labour)			Lib Dems (vs. Labour)			SNP (vs. Labour)		
	B	s.e.	p =	B	s.e.	p =	B	s.e.	p =
Age 18–34	-1.96	0.87	0.03	-0.57	1.11	0.61	0.06	0.61	0.92
Age 55–81	-0.30	0.51	0.56	0.76	0.67	0.26	-1.21	0.43	0.01
Men	0.20	0.52	0.70	-0.86	0.67	0.20	-0.62	0.38	0.10
Social Class A,B	-1.33	0.72	0.07	-1.95	1.27	0.13	-0.89	0.61	0.15
Social Class C2, D, E	-1.87	0.63	0.00	-1.49	0.71	0.04	-0.50	0.45	0.26
Education, Vocational	1.90	1.11	0.09	-3.47	1.40	0.01	-0.51	0.84	0.54
Education, Standard Grade	0.11	0.86	0.90	-0.81	0.97	0.41	-2.01	0.54	0.00
Education, Highers	-0.11	0.74	0.89	-0.37	0.74	0.62	-1.50	0.60	0.01
Education, Degree	-0.24	0.87	0.78	0.23	0.97	0.81	-1.15	0.60	0.05
Religion, Catholic	-0.87	1.04	0.40	-5.31	1.49	0.00	-0.36	0.59	0.54
Religion, Church of Scotland	-1.10	0.62	0.08	0.20	0.82	0.81	-0.61	0.54	0.26
Religion, Other Protestant	-0.57	0.87	0.51	-0.86	1.02	0.40	-1.59	0.64	0.01
Religion, Others	1.11	1.64	0.50	2.27	1.18	0.05	-0.33	1.82	0.86
Tabloid readers	-1.21	0.85	0.15	-1.04	0.92	0.26	0.52	0.66	0.43
Broadsheet readers	-0.16	0.80	0.84	-1.17	0.88	0.18	0.51	0.63	0.42
Urban resident	-0.17	0.52	0.74	-0.04	0.62	0.95	-0.39	0.46	0.40
Employed in private sector	-0.19	0.53	0.72	-0.49	0.67	0.46	0.20	0.41	0.64
Trade union member	0.68	0.49	0.16	0.67	0.60	0.27	1.77	0.37	0.00
Support community sentences	-0.18	0.23	0.42	-0.60	0.33	0.07	-0.18	0.17	0.28
Oppose free prescriptions	0.42	0.18	0.02	0.53	0.21	0.01	0.23	0.13	0.09

More use of tax-varying powers	0.62	0.23	0.01	0.16	0.24	0.49	0.57	0.19	0.00
Support prison for knife crime	-0.77	0.23	0.00	-0.51	0.31	0.09	-0.65	0.17	0.00
Support tuition fees	-0.19	0.24	0.43	-0.36	0.24	0.14	-0.07	0.17	0.68
Oppose spending cuts	0.22	0.27	0.42	0.08	0.34	0.83	0.10	0.20	0.63
Tax-spend scale (increase)	-0.13	0.14	0.38	-0.19	0.17	0.25	-0.05	0.11	0.68
Green vs. growth scale (growth)	0.33	0.14	0.02	-0.11	0.17	0.51	0.02	0.11	0.89
Constitution scale (independence)	0.20	0.12	0.10	0.01	0.14	0.97	0.28	0.09	0.00
Standards of health	-0.40	0.33	0.23	-0.21	0.41	0.62	0.05	0.23	0.83
Standards of education	-0.14	0.35	0.69	0.14	0.48	0.77	0.04	0.27	0.88
Living standards	0.12	0.31	0.71	0.03	0.44	0.95	-0.03	0.23	0.89
Standards of law and order	0.39	0.39	0.32	0.32	0.51	0.53	-0.18	0.33	0.59
Con UK performance	0.84	0.43	0.05	0.54	0.45	0.23	0.58	0.31	0.06
Lib Dem UK performance	0.28	0.41	0.49	-0.19	0.51	0.70	-0.27	0.37	0.46
Lab UK performance	0.00	0.38	0.99	0.28	0.58	0.63	0.02	0.32	0.95
SNP Sco performance	0.62	0.36	0.09	0.74	0.45	0.10	2.16	0.37	0.00
Lab Sco performance	-1.44	0.41	0.00	-1.14	0.54	0.04	-1.66	0.38	0.00
Prospective evaluation – UK economy	0.18	0.34	0.61	0.14	0.53	0.80	0.31	0.24	0.20
Prospective evaluation – Scottish economy	-0.01	0.35	0.97	0.16	0.56	0.78	0.36	0.26	0.17
Handle cuts – Conservatives	0.72	0.44	0.10	-0.98	0.63	0.12	-0.32	0.30	0.28
Handle cuts – Labour	-0.44	0.54	0.42	-0.08	0.65	0.91	-0.91	0.44	0.04
Handle cuts – Lib Dems	-0.07	0.50	0.89	1.54	0.85	0.07	-0.33	0.34	0.34
Handle cuts – SNP	0.19	0.49	0.70	-0.71	0.77	0.35	0.14	0.40	0.73
Alex Salmond	-0.10	0.14	0.49	0.01	0.12	0.94	0.47	0.12	0.00
Iain Gray	-0.16	0.15	0.27	-0.44	0.19	0.02	0.01	0.11	0.96
Annabel Goldie	0.15	0.11	0.19	-0.40	0.13	0.00	-0.12	0.08	0.14
Tavish Scott	0.06	0.16	0.68	0.66	0.23	0.00	0.02	0.12	0.90
David Cameron	0.46	0.17	0.01	0.12	0.20	0.54	0.20	0.11	0.06

Table A2 6.1 (Continued)

	Conservative (vs. Labour)			Lib Dems (vs. Labour)			SNP (vs. Labour)		
	B	s.e.	P =	B	s.e.	P =	B	s.e.	P =
Nick Clegg	-0.27	0.16	0.09	-0.07	0.18	0.69	-0.05	0.12	0.65
Ed Miliband	-0.41	0.15	0.01	-0.22	0.19	0.25	-0.22	0.11	0.04
Gordon Brown	-0.21	0.11	0.07	0.06	0.18	0.72	-0.30	0.10	0.00
Tony Blair	-0.11	0.10	0.25	-0.10	0.13	0.47	-0.19	0.08	0.01
Party image – Conservatives	1.00	0.30	0.00	0.12	0.38	0.76	0.18	0.24	0.46
Party image – Labour	-0.45	0.33	0.18	-0.95	0.40	0.02	-0.54	0.27	0.04
Party image – Lib Dems	0.01	0.33	0.97	1.31	0.41	0.00	0.27	0.24	0.27
Party image – SNP	0.32	0.39	0.40	-0.06	0.41	0.88	0.45	0.30	0.14
Scottish interests – Conservatives	0.16	0.41	0.00	-0.34	0.54	0.53	0.31	0.31	0.33
Scottish interests – Labour	-1.48	0.51	0.00	-2.15	0.71	0.00	-1.94	0.45	0.00
Scottish interests – Lib Dems	-0.74	0.49	0.13	1.86	0.76	0.02	0.46	0.31	0.14
Scottish interests – SNP	0.94	0.36	0.01	0.85	0.48	0.08	0.99	0.34	0.00
Campaign tone – Conservatives	0.62	0.35	0.08	-0.10	0.40	0.80	-0.05	0.23	0.81
Campaign tone – Labour	-0.43	0.35	0.22	-1.61	0.56	0.00	-0.29	0.23	0.19
Campaign tone – Lib Dems	0.64	0.27	0.02	0.98	0.36	0.01	-0.10	0.23	0.68
Campaign tone – SNP	0.40	0.29	0.17	0.43	0.30	0.14	0.30	0.21	0.15
Constant	2.86	4.78	0.55	1.71	5.90	0.77	-4.01	4.01	0.32

N = 1211 Pseudo R² = .80
Coefficients in bold p ≤ .05

Notes

2 Results and the Sources of Party Support

1. We recognize, of course that church attendance is not the most precise measure of religiosity. That said, given data limitations owing to questionnaire length, we were unable to include a more extensive battery of questions assessing religiosity. That said, there is plenty of support for our approach in the existing literature (Green 2010).
2. In the 2011 SES, the 'Moreno question' took the form, 'Which, if any, of the following best describes how you see yourself?', with the response options:

    Scottish not British
    More Scottish than British
    Equally Scottish and British
    More British than Scottish
    British not Scottish

    Respondents were also permitted to respond 'Other' (and given an open text box to describe themselves) or 'Don't Know'.
3. That is, the variable indicating a voter's vote choice contains a series of categories in which we can indicate whether a person opted to vote for the Conservatives, Labour, Liberal Democrats, SNP, Greens or some other party. These are discrete and mutually exclusive categories – a voter could not (legally) vote for both Labour and the Liberal Democrats on their list ballot.

3 Parties and Leaders

1. Evidence submitted by Ian Small, Head of Public Policy & Corporate Affairs, BBC Scotland, to Education and Culture Committee, 24 January 2012, paper EC/S4/12/21.

4 Performance Politics at Holyrood

1. We also exclude the 3 per cent who misinterpreted the question as one about how or why they cast a vote at all (citing civic duty or the merits of a postal vote, for example).
2. The 'Public finances' category inevitably includes both those lamenting the size of the deficit (many of whom named the Conservatives as the best-equipped party) and those lamenting the cuts planned to deal with it (who were split fairly evenly between Labour and the SNP).

3. The issue statements are taken from the Scottish Vote Compass (see Wheatley et al. forthcoming), an online Voting Advice Application available to Scottish voters in the run-up to the 2011 election. This recorded voters' policy preferences and matched them to the parties' offerings at this election. Since it is explicitly designed to probe those areas on which the parties disagree, it is a useful guide to the position issues that were at least potentially in play at this election.

4. The five options are as follows:

   - Scotland should become independent, separate from the UK and the European Union.
   - Scotland should become independent, separate from the UK but part of the European Union.
   - Scotland should remain part of the UK, with its own elected parliament which has some taxation powers.
   - Scotland should remain part of the UK, with its own elected parliament, which has no taxation powers.
   - Scotland should remain part of the UK without an elected parliament.

   The 2011 SES question is phrased a little differently, clarifying that the status quo involves some but limited taxation powers, but is similar enough to be regarded as broadly comparable. The slightly amended options are:

   - Scotland should be independent outside the European Union.
   - Scotland should be independent within the European Union.
   - The Scottish Parliament's powers should be increased and it should raise more of its own taxes.
   - There should be no change to the present arrangements: Scotland should have a devolved Parliament with limited powers.
   - The Scottish Parliament should be abolished and all Scottish laws passed by Westminster again.

5. Age, sex and education were also included in the model as control variables but are not shown in Figure 4.2 because their effects are not the main concern here. The full model, including all parameter estimates, error variances and measures of fit, is presented in Appendix 2 Table A2 4.1.

5   How 'Scottish' Was this Election?

1. The nature of this question, asking about the 'present time', discourages mentions of longstanding issues like the constitutional question. So Table 5.3 should not be read as implying that independence was unimportant in the 2011 election. Table 4.1 already contradicts that idea. However, the results in this chapter show the potential for short-term concerns like the economy in 2011 to overshadow those more enduring concerns.

2. A parallel result is obtained by broadening this analysis beyond the economy to a comparison based on the full range of issues. Cramer's V

summarizes the similarities between the 'most important issue when voting' responses and each of the multi-level measures, and the coefficient is 0.31 – at most a moderate association – for both the 'facing Britain' and 'facing Scotland' questions. Again, the obvious conclusion is that some voters were driven by British considerations while others were focused on the Scottish level.

3. There was an 'Other reasons' option offered but, since our principal concern is with the relative importance of British and Scottish levels, we omit that third option in analysis here.

4. It hardly needs saying – and so we did not report in Table 5.5 – that those referring explicitly to 'Scotland', 'Scottish interests', or the record of the Scottish government when asked the most important issue question were also overwhelmingly likely to report a vote focused mostly on what was going on in Scotland. More important is that they far outnumber those whose 'most important issue' response referred to the British level (e.g. criticizing the government or the parties at Westminster). This reinforces the first-order credentials of the 2011 election.

5. Given that above we reported that there were some differences in response patterns discernible across the two halves, we would caution that these measures of multi-level party support should be viewed with some degree of scepticism. While the differences in response patterns were slight enough that we feel we can broadly characterise party support at the Scottish and UK levels, there will be measurement error in these measures.

6 Party Choice in 2011

1. We adopt a relatively relaxed criterion for significance, $p < 0.1$, because the small cell sizes in such a full specification – especially when predicting votes for the Conservatives and the Liberal Democrats –mean that even relatively strong substantive effects sometimes fall short of the more standard $p < 0.05$ statistical significance requirement.

2. This introduces a slight bias because, other things remaining the same, a full-range change on an 11-point scale is a more dramatic shift than the corresponding change on a 4-point scale. However, eliminating this bias is only possible with much less intuitive statistics such as the effect of moving one standard deviation along a scale. Here we opt for the simpler version; Johns et al. (2013), using the more complex approach, reach identical substantive conclusions.

References

Abedi, A. and A. Siaroff (1999). 'The mirror has broken: Increasing divergence between national and land elections in Austria', *German Politics*, 8: 207–227.

Anderson, B. (1991). *Imagined communities: Reflections on the origin and spread of nationalism*, London: Verso.

Anderson, C. D. (2006). 'Economic voting and multilevel governance: A comparative individual-level analysis', *American Journal of Political Science*, 50(2): 449–463.

Andersen, R. and Evans, G. (2003). 'Who Blairs wins? Leadership and voting in the 2001 election', *British Elections & Parties Review*, 13, 229–247.

Arceneaux, K. (2006). 'The federal face of voting: Are elected officials held accountable for the functions relevant to their office?' *Political Psychology*, 27(5): 731–754.

Bartolini, S. and P. Mair (1990). *Identity, competition and electoral availability: The stabilization of European electorates 1885–1985*, Cambridge: Cambridge University Press.

Bennie, L., J. Brand and J. Mitchell (1997). *How Scotland votes*, Manchester: Manchester University Press.

Beveridge, C. (2010). *Report of the Independent budget review panel*, available online at: www.scotland.gov.uk/Resource/Doc/919/0102335.pdf

Black, R. (2010). Letter to independent budget review panel, June, quoted in C. Beveridge (2010), *Report of the independent budget review panel*, available online at: www.scotland.gov.uk/Resource/Doc/919/0102335.pdf.

Blake, D. (1982). 'The consistency of inconsistency: Party identification in Federal provincial politics', *Canadian Journal of Political Science*, 15: 691–710.

Blake, D. with D. Elkins and R. Johnston (1985). *Two political worlds: Parties and voting in British Columbia*, Vancouver: University of British Columbia Press.

Bochel, J. and D. Denver (1970). 'Religion and voting: A critical review and a new analysis', *Political Studies*, 18: 205–219.

Brand, J., J. Mitchell and P. Surridge (1993). 'Identity and the vote: Class and nationality in Scotland', in D. Denver, P. Norris, D. Broughton and C. Rallings (eds.), *British elections and parties yearbook*, Hemel Hempstead, Herts: Harvester Wheatsheaf, 143–157.

Brickman, P., V. C. Rabinowitz, D. Coates, E. Cohn, and L. Kidder (1982). 'Models of helping and coping', *American Psychologist*, 37: 364–384.

Bromley, C., J. Curtice, D. McCrone and A. Park (eds.) (2006) *Has devolution delivered?* Edinburgh: Edinburgh University Press.

Brown, A. (2000). 'Designing the Scottish Parliament', *Parliamentary Affairs*, 53: 542–556

Brown, A., D. McCrone and L. Paterson (1996). *Politics and society in Scotland*, Basingstoke: MacMillan Press.

Brown, A., D. McCrone, L. Paterson and P. Surridge (1999) *The Scottish electorate*, Basingstoke: Macmillan.

Budge, I. and D. Urwin (1966). *Scottish political behaviour: A case study in British homogeneity*, London: Longman.

Budge, I., J. Brand, M. Margolis and A. Smith (1972). *Political stratification and democracy*, London: Macmillan.

Burden, B. C. and C. A. Klofstad (2005). 'Affect and cognition in party identification', *Political Psychology*, 26(6): 869–886.

Butler, D. (2008). 'Hung parliaments: Context and background' in A. Brazier and S. Kilitowski (eds.), *No overall control? The impact of a 'hung parliament' on British politics*, London: Hansard Society.

Butler, D. and R. Rose (1960). *The British General Election of 1959*. London: Macmillan.

Butler, D. and D. Stokes (1974). *Political change in Britain: The evolution of electoral choice*, London: Macmillan.

Butt, S. (2006). 'How Voters Evaluate Economic Competence: A Comparison between Parties In and Out of Power.' *Political Studies* 54: 743–766.

Campbell, A., P. Converse, W. Miller and D. Stokes (1960). *The American voter*, Chicago: University of Chicago Press.

Carman, C., J. Mitchell and R. Johns (2008). 'The unfortunate natural experiment in ballot design: The Scottish parliamentary elections of 2007', *Electoral Studies*, 27: 442–459.

Clarke, Harold D. and Allan McCutcheon (2009). The dynamics of party identification reconsidered. *Public Opinion Quarterly*, 73: 704–728.

Clarke, H. D. and M. C. Stewart (1998). 'The decline of parties in the minds of citizens', *Annual Review of Political Science*, 1: 357–378.

Clarke, H. D., D. Sanders, M. C. Stewart and P. Whiteley (2004). *Political choice in Britain*. Oxford: Oxford University Press.

Clarke, H., D. Sanders, M. Stewart, and P. Whiteley (2011). 'Valence politics and electoral choice in Britain, 2010', *Journal of Elections, Public Opinion & Parties*, 21(2): 237–253.

Clarke, H. D., D. Sanders, M. C. Stewart and P. Whiteley (2009). *Performance politics and the British voter*. Cambridge: Cambridge University Press.

Converse, P. (1964) 'The nature of belief systems in mass publics' in D. Apter (ed.): *Ideology and discontent*, London: Free Press of Glencoe, 206–261.

Copeland, G. and S. Patterson (1994). 'Changing an institutionalized setting' in G. Copeland and S. Patterson (eds.) *Parliaments in the modern world*, Ann Arbor: Michigan University Press.

Curtice, J. (2006). 'Is Holyrood accountable and representative?' in C. Bromley, J. Curtice, D. McCrone and A. Park (eds.) *Has devolution delivered?* Edinburgh: Edinburgh University Press, pp. 90–122.

Curtice, J. and S. Holmberg (2005). 'Leaders', in J. Thomassen (ed.) *The European voter: A comparative study of modern democracies*, Oxford: Oxford University Press, pp. 125–166.

Curtice, J., D. McCrone, N. McEwen, M. Marsh, and R. Ormston (2009) *Revolution or evolution? The 2007 Scottish elections*. Edinburgh: Edinburgh University Press.

Cutler, F. (2004). 'Government responsibility and electoral accountability in federations', *Publius*, 34(1): 19–38.

Cutler, F. (2008). 'Whodunnit? voters and responsibility in Canadian federalism', *Canadian Journal of Political Science*, 41: 627–654.

Crewe, I. (1982). 'Is Britain's two-party system really about to crumble?', *Electoral Studies*, 1: 275–314.

Crewe, I. (1988). 'Partisan alignment ten years on' in Berrington, H. (ed.), *Change in British politics*. London: Frank Cass.

Crewe, I., B. Sarlvik and J. Alt (1977). 'Partisan dealignment in Britain, 1964–1974', *British Journal of Political Science*, 7: 129–190.

Dalton, R. (1996). *Citizen politics: Public opinion and political parties in advanced western democracies*, Chatham NJ: Chatham House Publishers.

Dalton, R. (2002). 'Political cleavages, issues, and electoral change' in L. Le Duc, R.G. Niemi and P. Norris (eds.), *Comparing democracies 2: New challenges in the study of elections and voting*, Thousand Oaks, CA: Sage.

Dalton, R. (2006). *Citizen politics: Public opinion and political parties in advanced western democracies*, 4th ed., Washington, DC: CQ Press.

Dalton, Russell J. and Martin P. Wattenberg (eds.) (2000). *Parties without partisans*. Oxford: Oxford University Press.

Delli Carpini, X. Michael and Scott Keeter (1996). *What Americans know about politics and why it matters*. New Haven: Yale University Press.

Denver, D., C. Carman and R. Johns (2012). *Elections and voters in Britain*, 3rd ed. Basingstoke: Palgrave.

Denver, D. and R. Johns (2010). 'Scottish Parliament elections: "British not Scottish" or "More Scottish than British"?' *Scottish Affairs*, 70(1): 9–28.

Denver, D., J. Mitchell, C. Pattie, and H. Bochel (2000). *Scotland decides: The devolution issue and the 1997 referendum*, London: Frank Cass.

Dewar, D. (1999). 'Speech to Labour Party conference,' 27 September, available online at: http://news.bbc.co.uk/1/hi/uk_politics/459041.stm Downs, Anthony (1957). *An economic theory of democracy*. New York: Harper & Row.

Downs, A. (1962). *The theory of political coalitions*, New Haven, CT: Yale University Press.

Duch, R.M. and R.T. Stevenson (2008). *The economic vote: How political and economic institutions condition election results*, Cambridge: Cambridge University Press.

Dunleavy, P. (2005). 'Facing up to multi-party politics: How partisan dealignment and PR voting have fundamentally changed Britain's party systems', *Parliamentary Affairs*, 58(3): 503–532.

Electoral Commission (2012). *Scottish Parliament Election 2011: Campaign expenditure*, Edinburgh, Electoral Commission.

Elff, M. (2007). 'Social structure and electoral behavior in comparative perspective: The decline of social cleavages in western Europe revisited', *Perspectives on Politics*, 5: 277–294.

Erikson, R.S. (1988). 'The puzzle of midterm loss', *Journal of Politics*, 50: 1011–1029.

Evans, G. and R. Andersen (2005). 'The impact of party leaders: How Blair lost Labour votes' in P. Norris and C. Wlezien (eds.), *Britain Votes 2005*, Oxford: Oxford University Press, 162–180.

Fieldhouse, E. and A. Russell (2001). 'Latent Liberals? Sympathy and support for the Liberal Democrats in Britain', *Party Politics*, 7: 711–738.

Fiorina, M. (1981). *Retrospective voting in American national election*, New Haven: Yale University Press.

Flanagan, S. (1987). 'Value change in industrial society,' *American Political Science Review*, 81: 1303–1319.

Foley, Michael. (1993). *The Rise of British Presidency*, Manchester: Manchester University Press.

Franklin, M. (1985). *The decline of class voting in Britain: Changes in the basis of electoral choice, 1964–1983*, Oxford: Clarendon Press.

Franklin, M.N., T.T. Mackie and H. Valen (1992). *Electoral change: Response to evolving social and attitudinal structures in Western countries*, Cambridge: Cambridge University Press.

Friedman, T. (1999). *The Lexus and the Olive tree: Understanding globalisation*, Anchor Books.

Gallagher, M., M. Laver, and P. Mair, (2006). *Representative government in modern Europe*, New York: McGraw-Hill.

Green, J. (2007). 'When voters and parties agree: Valence issues and party competition', *Political Studies*, 55 (3): 629–655.

Green, J.C. (2010). "Gauging the God Gap: Religion and Voting in US Presidential Elections," in J E Leighley (ed.), *The Oxford Handbook of American Elections and Political Behavior*, Oxford: Oxford University Press.

Green, Donald P., Bradley Palmquist and Eric Schickler (2002). *Partisan Hearts and Minds*. New Haven, CT: Yale University Press.

Green-Pederson, C. (2001). 'Minority governments and party politics: The political and institutional background to the "Danish Miracle" ', *Journal of Public Policy*, 21: 53–70.

Heath, A.F., R. Jowell and J. Curtice (2001). *The rise of new labour*, Oxford: Oxford University Press.

Heath, A.F., and S.K. MacDonald (1987). 'Social change and the future of the left', *Political Quarterly*, 58: 364–377.

Heath, A., I. McLean, B. Taylor and J. Curtice (1999). 'Between first and second order: A comparison of voting behaviour in European and local elections in Britain', *European Journal of Political Research*, 35: 389–414.

Held, D. and A. McGrew (1998) 'The end of the old order? Globalization and the prospects for world order,' *Review of International Studies*, 24(5): 219–254.

Hellwig, T. (2008). 'Globalization, policy constraints, and vote choice', *Journal of Politics*, 70: 1128–1141.

Henderson, A. and N. McEwen (2010). 'A comparative analysis of voter turnout in regional elections', *Electoral Studies*, 29: 405–416.

Horsman, M. and A. Marshall (1994). *After the nation state*, London: HarperCollins.

Hough, D. and C. Jeffrey (2006). *Devolution and electoral politics*, Manchester: Manchester University Press.

Howat, B. (2006). *Choices for a purpose: Review of Scottish executive budgets, report of the budget review group*, available online at: www.scotland.gov.uk/Resource/Doc/178289/0050741.pdf13

Inglehart, R. (1977). *The Silent revolution: Changing values and political styles among Western publics*, Princeton, NJ: Princeton University Press.

Inglehart, R. (1999). 'Postmodernization, authority and democracy', in P. Norris (ed.) *Critical citizens*, Oxford: Oxford University Press.

Iyengar, S. (1989). *News that matters: Television and American opinion*, Chicago: University of Chicago Press.

Jennings, K. and R. Niemi (1966). 'Party identification at multiple levels of governments,' *American Journal of Sociology*, 72(1): 86–101.

Johns, R. (2011). 'Credit where it's due? Valence politics, attributions of responsibility, and multi-level elections', *Political Behavior*, 33(1): 53–77.

Johns, R., L. Bennie and J. Mitchell (2011). 'Gendered nationalism? The gender gap in support for the Scottish National Party', *Party Politics*, 18: 581–601.

Johns, R., C.J. Carman and J. Mitchell (2013). 'Constitution or competence? The SNP's re-election in 2011', *Political Studies*, 61(S1): 158–78.

Johns, R., D. Denver, J. Mitchell, and C. Pattie (2007). SES 2007: Comparison of face-to-face and internet samples. Unpublished paper.

Johns, R., D. Denver, J. Mitchell, and C. Pattie (2009). 'Valence politics in Scotland: Towards an explanation of the 2007 election', *Political Studies*, 57(1): 207–233.

Johns, R., J. Mitchell, D. Denver, and C. Pattie (2010). *Voting for a Scottish Government: The Scottish Parliament Elections of 2007*, Manchester: Manchester University Press.

Johnston, R. (2006). 'Party identification: Unmoved mover or sum of preferences?' *Annual Review of Political Science*, 9: 329–351.

Jones, R.W and R. Scully (2008). 'The end of one-partyism? Party politics in Wales in the second decade of devolution,' *Contemporary Wales*, 21: 207–217.

Katz, R. (1997). *Democracy and elections*, Oxford: Oxford University Press.

Kemmelmeier, M. and D. Winter (2008). 'Sowing patriotism, but reaping nationalism? Consequences of exposure to the American flag'. *Political Psychology*, 29(6): 859–879.

Key, V. O. (1966). *The responsible electorate*. Cambridge, MA: Belknap.

King, A. (2002). 'Do leaders' personalities really matter?', in Anthony King (ed), *Leaders' personalities and the outcomes of democratic elections*, Oxford: Oxford University Press.

Kirchheimer, O. (1966). 'The transformation of Western European Party Systems', in J. LaPalombara and M. Weiner (eds.), *Political parties and political development*, Princeton: Princeton University Press.

Lazarsfeld, P., B. Berelson, and H. Gaudet (1968). *The people's choice*, New York: Columbia University Press.

León, S. (2010). 'Who is responsible for what? Clarity of responsibility in multilevel systems. The case of Spain', *European Journal of Political Research*, 50: 80–109.

León, S. (2011). 'How does decentralization affect electoral competition of state-wide parties? Evidence from Spain', *Party Politics*, online, 80–109.

Lipset S.M. and S. Rokkan (eds.) (1967). *Party systems and voter alignments: Cross-national perspectives*, London: Collier-Macmillan.

Lodge, Milton, and Charles S. Taber (2013). *The rationalizing voter*. New York: Cambridge University Press.

Miller, W. (1981). *The end of British politics*, Oxford: Clarendon Press.

Miller, A. E., M.P. Wattenberg, and O. Malanchuk, (1986). 'Schematic assessments of presidential candidates', *American Political Science Review*, 80: 521–540.

McLean. I., A. Heath and B. Taylor (1996). 'Were the 1994 Euro- and local elections in Britain really second order? Evidence from the British election panel study', *Journal of Elections, Public Opinion and Parties*, 6: 1–20.

Mitchell, J. (2010). 'Two models of devolution: A framework of analysis' in K. Stolz (ed.), *Ten years of devolution in the United Kingdom*, Augsburg: Wissner-Verlag.

Mitchell, James (1990). *Conservatives and the union*, Edinburgh, Edinburgh University Press.

Mitchell, J. (2010b). 'The Narcissism of small differences: Scotland and Westminster', *Parliamentary Affairs*, 63: 98–116.

Mitchell, J., R. Johns and L. Bennie (2011). *The Scottish National Party: Transition to Power*, Oxford University Press.

Mughan, Anthony (2000). *Media and the Presidentialisation of Parliamentary Elections*, Houndmills, Basingstoke: Macmillan.

Nannestad, P. and M. Paldam (1994). 'The VP-function: A survey of the literature on vote and popularity functions after 25 Years', *Public Choice*, 79(3–4): 213–245.

Nice, D. and P. Fredericksen (1996). *The politics of intergovernmental relations*, Chicago: Nelson-Hall Publishers.

Ohmae, K. (1990). *The borderless world*, London: Collins.

Osmond, J. (2005). 'Provenance and promise' in J. Osmond (ed.), *Welsh Politics come of age*, Cardiff: Institute of Welsh Politics.

Paterson, L. (2006). 'Sources of support for the SNP' in C. Bromley, J. Curtice, D. McCrone and A. Park (eds.), *Has devolution delivered?* Edinburgh: Edinburgh University Press, 46–68.

Paterson, L., A. Brown, J. Curtice, K. Hinds, D. McCrone, A. Park, K. Sproston and P. Surridge (2001). *New Scotland, new politics?* Edinburgh: Polygon.

Pattie, C., D. Denver, R. Johns, and J. Mitchell (2011). 'Raising the tone? The impact of 'positive' and 'negative' campaigning on voting in the 2007 Scottish Parliament election', *Electoral Studies*, 30: 333–343.

Peres, H. (2007). 'Genèse et contexte d'une invention : le questionnaire de Juan Linz entre identité subjective et prétentions nationalistes', *Revue internationale de politique compare*, 14: 515–530.

Powell, G.B. (2000). *Elections as instruments of democracy: Majoritarian and proportional visions*, New Haven, CT: Yale University Press.

Quinn, Thomas (2008) 'The conservative party and the 'centre ground' of British politics', *Journal of Elections, Public Opinion and Parties*, 18(2): 177–199.

Reif, K. and H. Schmitt (1980). 'Nine second-order national elections: A conceptual framework for the analysis of European election results', *European Journal of Political Research*, 8: 3–44.

Rose, R. (1974). 'Comparability in electoral studies', in R. Rose (ed.), *Electoral behaviour: A comparative handbook*, New York: The Free Press.

Rose, R. and D. Urwin (1969). 'Persistence and change in Western Party systems since 1945', *Political Studies*, 18: 287–319.

Rose, R. and D. Urwin (1970). 'Social cohesion, political parties and strains in regimes', *Comparative Political Studies*, 2: 7–67.

Scarrow, S. (2000). 'Parties without members? Party organization in a changing electoral environment,' in R. Dalton and M. Wattenberg (eds.), *Parties without Partisans: Political change in advanced industrial democracies*, Oxford: Oxford University Press.

Scully, R. and A. Elias (2008). 'The 2007 Welsh Assembly Elections', *Regional and Federal Studies*, 18: 103–109.

Scholte, J.A. (2000). *Globalisation: A critical introduction*, London: Macmillan.

Schuman, H. and S. Presser (1996). *Questions and answers in attitude surveys*. London: Sage.

SNP and Greens (2007). 'Scottish National Party & Scottish Green Party Cooperation Agreement', available online at: http://news.bbc.co.uk/1/shared/bsp/hi/pdfs/11_05_07_agreement.pdf.

Stevens, D., J. Karp, and R. Hodgson (2011) 'Party leaders as movers and shakers in British campaigns? Results from the 2010 election', *Journal of Elections, Public Opinion & Parties*, 21 (2), 125–145.

Stewart, M.C. and H.D. Clarke (1998). 'The dynamics of Party identification in Federal Systems: The Canadian Case,' *American Journal of Political Science*, 42 (1): 97–116.

Strøm, K. (1990). *Minority Government and Majority Rule*, Cambridge: Cambridge University Press.

Stokes, D. (1963). 'Spatial models of party competition', *American Political Science Review*, 57: 368–377.

Stokes, D. (1992). 'Valence politics', in D. Kavanagh (ed.), *Electoral politics*. Oxford: Clarendon.

Studlar, D. (2001). 'Canadian exceptionalism: Explaining differences over time in provincial and federal voter turnout', *Canadian Journal of Political Science*, 34: 299–319.

Surridge, P. (2006). 'A better union?' in C. Bromley, J. Curtice, D. McCrone and A. Park (eds.), *Has devolution delivered?* Edinburgh: Edinburgh University Press, 29–45.

Tilley, James (2003).' Party identification in Britain: Does length of time in the electorate affect strength of partisanship?' *British Journal of Political Science,* 33(2): 332–344.

Tufte, E. (1978). *Political control of the economy,* Princeton: Princeton University Press.

Vowles, J. (2008). 'Does globalization affect public perceptions of "Who in power can make a difference"? Evidence from 40 countries, 1996–2006', *Electoral Studies,* 27: 63–76.

Vowles, J. (2010). 'Making a difference? Public perceptions of coalition, single-party, and minority governments', *Electoral Studies,* 29(3): 370–380.

Weiss, L. (1998). *The myth of the powerless state,* Cambridge: Polity Press.

Weiss, L. (ed.) (2003). *Studies in the global economy: Bringing domestic institutions back in,* Cambridge: Cambridge University.

Wheatley, J., Christopher Carman, Fernando Mendez, J. Mitchell, 'The dimensionality of the Scottish political space: Results from an experiment on the 2011 Holyrood elections', *Party Politics* forthcoming

Whiteley, P. (2009). 'Is the party over? The decline of party activism and membership across the democratic world,' Paper Presented at the Annual Meeting of the Poltical Studies Association, University of Manchester.

Wilson, T.D. (2004). *Strangers to ourselves: Discovering the adaptive unconscious,* Cambridge: Harvard University Press.

Wlezien, Christopher (2005). 'On the salience of political issues: The problem with "most important problem"'. *Electoral Studies* 24: 555–579.

Wyn Jones, R. and R. Scully (2006). 'Devolution and electoral politics in Scotland and Wales', *Publius,* 36: 115–134.

Zaller, John R. (1992). *The Nature and Origins of Mass Opinion.* New York: Cambridge University Press.

Zuckerman, A. (2005). 'Returning to the social logic of political behaviour', in A. Zuckerman (ed.), *The social logic of politics: Personal networks as contexts for political behaviour,* Philadelphia, PA: Temple University Press.

Index

Note: Page numbers in *italic* refer to tables; page numbers in **bold** refer to figures

Printed and bound in the United States of America